Ignite Your Career Journey with Confid

THRIVE AND SHINE

A Practical Guidebook for Early-Stage Professionals

JULEE SUNG

Lucky Book Publishing

Published by Lucky Book Publishing: www.luckybookpublishing.com

The author does not dispense medical advice or prescribe the use of any technique as a form of treatment for physical, emotional or medical problems without the advice of a physician, either directly or indirectly. The intent of the author is only to offer information of a general true nature to help you in your quest for emotional, physical and spiritual well-being. In the event you use any of the information in this book for yourself, the author and the publisher assume no responsibility for your actions.

To request permissions, contact the publisher at hello@luckybookpublishing.com.

Paperback ISBN: 978-1-998287-75-8
Hardcover ISBN: 978-1-998287-76-5
E-book ISBN: 978-1-998287-77-2

First edition, May 2025

My Gratitude Gift to You

I'm beyond thrilled that you're here!

As my gratitude gift to you,
get FREE Access to the Audiobook of Thrive and SHINE by scanning the QR Code below or by visiting https://www.juleesung.com

Praise for THRIVE AND SHINE

A Practical Guidebook for Early-Stage Professionals

Insight into Action!

Theory matters, but execution wins. This book helps you turn insight into action. Every college grad and anyone building their career should read it.

- **Dr. Timothy Chou, Stanford University Lecturer, Board Director, Chairman of Alchemist Accelerator, Founder & CEO of BevelCloud Inc.**

Very impactful!

Throughout my experience building and scaling organizations, I've consistently seen the transformative impact of individuals who take ownership of their growth. Julee exemplifies this through her remarkable creativity, unwavering drive, and genuine passion for helping others succeed. *Thrive and SHINE* is a reflection of the insight, dedication, and vision she has brought to her own career. It is an invaluable resource for anyone embarking on their professional journey.

- **Wendy Petty, Chief Revenue Officer at WorkFusion**

☆ Empowering, actionable, and full of heart!

Uplifting, honest, and deeply relatable, *Thrive and SHINE* is a must-read for anyone navigating the twists of early career life. With warmth and wisdom, Julee offers practical tools, inspiring case studies, and a refreshing reminder that showing up as your true self is your greatest strength. Empowering, actionable, and full of heart.

– **David Michael Slater, Author of *The Vanishing, Ugly*, and other fiction titles; Fiction Editor at JUDITH magazine**

☆ Brilliant!

Julee understands what it takes to grow into your potential at work because she's lived it and helped others do the same. *Thrive and SHINE* is a smart, down-to-earth guide for anyone who wants to build a career with integrity, confidence, and purpose.

– **Mike deFisser, Founder and CEO of FireOneCXO Partners**

☆ Establish a strong foundation for success!

Julee Sung has developed a fabulous toolbox that is accessible, clever, and empowering. Highly recommended for anyone who is launching (or relaunching) their career and wants to avoid common pitfalls, have greater insight into workplace culture, and establish a strong foundation for success, growth, and contribution!

– **Heather Hays, Associate Director at Los Angeles General Foundation**

Very resourceful for young career-oriented professionals.

A great tool for those who are just coming into the workforce and a great resource for the seasoned workers who need to fuel the spark once more. Julee shares her wisdom in a kind and effective way so the reader has quick access to the information and tips they are looking for.

- **Danielle C Baker, RECE, Author, TV & Podcast Host**

A must read!

Julee Sung's book, *Thrive and SHINE*, is transformative. It empowered me to embrace my unique entrepreneurial journey and ignore outside noise. The SHINE framework offers clarity, confidence, and authentic growth. A must-read!

- **Shelley Murdock, Author, IN SEARCH OF LONGEVITY, and HEALTHY & FIT FOR LIFE**

A down-to-earth guide for creating a good work life.

Julee's *Thrive and SHINE* really opened my eyes! It's a helpful, down-to-earth guide for creating a good work life. Julee's honest story and the SHINE steps felt real and made a big difference in how I see things. It's a book you'll keep coming back to for good ideas and to feel more sure of yourself as you build a career that feels right for you. I highly recommend it!

- **Manali Haridas, Spiritual Wellness Coach, Zen for You/ Author "You Got this Mom"**

Refreshingly Authentic!

At Fraktionals, we help companies align the right talent with the right stage, and I've seen firsthand how well early-career professionals thrive with the right guidance. In *Thrive and SHINE,* Julee's voice is clear, grounded, and refreshingly real—a smart, timely resource for anyone looking to grow with impact and intention.

- **Gabriela Gutiérrez, Founder at Fraktionals**

A guide that permits you to shine your unique light.

In both movement and life, true growth comes from embracing your authentic self. *Thrive and SHINE* is a heartfelt guide that encourages early-career professionals to trust their journey, embrace challenges, and shine in their own unique light.

- **Michèle Assaf, Producer and Artistic Director at World Dance Movement**

Thoughtful guidance that encourages growth with confidence.

Early in your career, it can feel like everyone expects you to have it all figured out. *Thrive and SHINE* offers the opposite: permission to be curious, to learn, and to build your path one step at a time. It's the kind of thoughtful guidance that helps people grow with confidence, not pressure.

- **Marion Lucarelli, Founder at Revenue Peak Services**

This book will empower you!

Julee brings a very effective and simple formula to follow in her book *Thrive and SHINE*. I loved the way it was structured and how she brings a bit of her personal story in each chapter, showing the reader how she needed to learn to empower herself through her career to have the success she has today. She is truly inspiring. I highly recommend this book.

- **Charles Achampong, Bestselling Author, *Around The World in Family Days***

A step by step guide to bring you to the best version of yourself!

If you really want to make a change in your workplace and start shining bright everyday, then this is the perfect book for you! *Thrive and SHINE* gives you a step by step guide to bring you to be the best version of yourself at work and to have the confidence to thrive by being YOU. There is so much value for those ready to take their power back and apply Julee's teachings.

- **Dionne Nicholls-Germain, Bestselling Author, *The 90-Day Conquering Unforgiveness Journal : For High-Performing High Achievers***

Great support for our young professionals!

Thrive and SHINE is such a remarkable guide for young professionals. It really brings the reader into pure authenticity and learning to own everything that you are. It is crucial in our society to continue to support young professionals in this way as they are the future and Julee sure nailed it in this book!

- **Teri Kingston, Bestselling Author, *Get Ready for Ted When Ted is Ready for You***

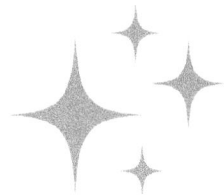

TABLE OF CONTENTS

MY DREAM

I wrote this book to light a spark—and to save you from learning *every* lesson the hard way. My dream is that these pages meet you right where you are, whether you're navigating a fresh start, chasing something bigger, or just trying to keep your head above water while figuring out what's next.

Thrive and SHINE is part pep talk, part strategy guide, part reality check. It's packed with real stories, hard-earned lessons, and the kind of encouragement that doesn't sugarcoat but still leaves you feeling like you've got this.

This isn't about being perfect or having it all figured out. It's about getting clear on who you are, trusting your instincts, and building a career (and life) that actually fits. With a little humor, a little heart, and a whole lot of honesty, this book is here to help you own your brilliance and shine on your own terms.

You're not just meant to survive. You're here to thrive—and shine while you're at it.

"I am not afraid of storms,

for I am learning how to sail my ship."

— Louisa May Alcott

Introduction

Step into Your Brilliance: Your Invitation to Thrive & SHINE

Welcome to the beautifully unpredictable world of building a career—full of growth, curveballs, unexpected wins, and the occasional "What am I even doing?" moment.

Whether you're stepping into your first role, shifting directions, or just trying to find your rhythm, this book is designed to help you move forward with more clarity, confidence, and intention.

I'm Julee. I've second-guessed decisions, chased gold stars, overworked to prove my worth—and I've also learned how to pause, pivot, and trust myself enough to chart a path that actually fits.

What I've learned along the way? Success isn't about flawless plans or picture-perfect progress. It's about navigating uncertainty, learning from the messy middle, and staying grounded in who you are as you grow.

That's where the **SHINE** framework comes in—a practical, personal guide to building a career that reflects your values, amplifies your strengths, and evolves with you.

Show Up Authentically – Let go of perfection, find your voice, and lead with clarity and confidence.

Harness Your Strengths – Know what you bring to the table—and use it intentionally.

Invest in Growth – Stay curious, take thoughtful risks, and turn both wins and stumbles into momentum.

Navigate Change – Adapt with resilience, set boundaries that support you, and make room for the unexpected.

Engage Meaningfully – Build connections that matter, receive feedback with grace, and cultivate a network that supports your growth.

Each chapter is filled with real stories, actionable takeaways, and honest reflections—offered with the hope that you'll feel less alone and more equipped as you move forward. You'll find lessons I've lived, missteps I've learned from, and insights I wish I'd had earlier.

There's no right way to read this book. Flip to what speaks to you. Reread when things feel uncertain. Skip around or move straight through—this is your space to reflect, reset, and reconnect with the kind of professional you want to be.

If you're ready to take the lead in your career and grow in a way that feels real, grounded, and fully your own...

Let's begin.
It's time to **Thrive & SHINE**.

Thrive and SHINE

S

Show Up Authentically

Welcome to the start of a journey that's all about you—not the polished, curated version you think you need to be, but the real, unfiltered, wildly capable person you already are. This isn't a manual for reinvention. It's a guide to owning your space, your voice, and your presence in a way that feels powerful, sustainable, and true.

Early in your career, it's tempting to believe that success is built on dazzling, high-impact moments. But real success is not just about the spotlight—it's about showing up consistently as your authentic self, even when no one's watching.

That's where this section comes in. Authenticity isn't about being the same in every situation—it's about knowing when and how to bring your best self forward. We'll explore how to balance professionalism with personality, how to stay true to your values without getting boxed in, and how to cultivate confidence without falling into perfectionism.

Here's the thing: You don't have to twist yourself into a version of success that doesn't fit. You just have to be you—mindfully.

Chapter 1

Show Up Every Day: Engage, Be Present, and Prioritize What Matters

Want to stand out? It's not about being the loudest or the flashiest—it's about being *present*. The workplace thrives on energy, commitment, and follow-through. People trust those who show up consistently, not just when it's convenient. But showing up fully doesn't mean exhausting yourself or overperforming—it's about being engaged in a way that's sustainable and impactful. The real magic happens when you're focused, intentional, and ready to contribute. Let's see how you can strike that balance between visibility and authenticity to make your presence count.

Confessions of a Polished Peg

For years, I felt like a square peg trying to jam myself into a round-hole corporate world. I didn't always match my colleagues' vibes, didn't share their career aspirations, and secretly wondered if at some point, someone would figure out I didn't belong.

So I did what many of us do: I smoothed my edges, played the part, and worked twice as hard to blend in. And for a while, I got away with it. But eventually, I hit a wall. Blending in wasn't the answer. The real game-changer? Owning my differences instead of burying them.

Why Presence is Your Career Superpower

★ **Your Presence Speaks Before You Do**
Being fully engaged signals reliability. People trust those who consistently show up—not just physically, but mentally. When you're dialed in, you build credibility, and credibility opens doors faster than a single moment of brilliance.

- **Engagement Sparks Unexpected Opportunities**

  When you're fully present, you notice gaps, trends, and chances others overlook. You see where you can add value, sharpen skills, and form connections that set you up for future success.

- **Proactive Energy Makes You Stand Out**

  Taking initiative, asking smart questions, and participating fully shows that you care about the bigger picture. That's what makes people remember you for the right reasons—not just as someone who was there, but as someone who made an impact.

- **Smart Prioritization Boosts Productivity**

  Showing up doesn't mean doing everything—it means focusing on what matters most. When you're fully present, you make smarter decisions about where to invest your energy instead of spreading yourself too thin.

- **Authenticity Over Ego Builds Lasting Trust**

  You don't need to prove yourself with flashy moments or forced confidence. Being genuinely engaged—listening, contributing thoughtfully, and owning your perspective—builds stronger, more meaningful connections over time.

My Own Lesson: Keeping It Real from Coast to Coast

When I landed a big promotion at my company's East Coast headquarters, it should've been a dream leap. But for the HQ crowd, it was more like an unwelcome disruption. There were plenty of viable candidates, and I was an unknown from the West swooping in. The culture was one of having to prove your worth, no benefit of the doubt given off the bat.

From day one, the culture shock was real. The office felt sharp-edged and closed off. Conversations were curt, no one asked questions, and certainly no one waited for my input.

I tried to adapt. I pulled on a tougher exterior, put on a brave face, and tried to blend in. I told myself I just needed to adapt. But nothing clicked. I wasn't connecting. I wasn't thriving. I was shrinking.

Then, after one particularly brutal day of stiff meetings and silent rejections, something cracked. I reminded myself: *They could have hired anyone for this job. But they hired you. For a reason.*

So I took off my HQ costume and started really showing up. I smiled big, asked questions, shared ideas—invited or not. I was determined to let my

California sunshine seep in everywhere. I didn't force anything and let my natural voice back in.

Then something shifted. People started responding. Conversations opened up. I started finding my rhythm.

It was still a big adjustment. I worked faster, sharpened my responses, learned how to navigate the pace. But I did it without trading in what made me different. That shift didn't just help me integrate at HQ—it helped me grow into the leader I was becoming.

The Lesson Earned

I thought I had to morph into some tougher, sharper, more "HQ-ready" version of myself to survive. But the truth? That version of me was exhausting and ineffective.

The moment I dropped the act and leaned into who I *really* was, things started to click. People stopped seeing me as an outsider and started responding. And the best part? I felt better. I wasn't bracing myself every day; I was finally *showing up*.

I used to think I had to blend in with the environment, but now I know it's about bringing all of myself to the table. Adapting is fine. Hiding isn't.

Case Study 1: From Lone Wolf to Leader

Stage Setting:

Sarah, a newly appointed team lead in software support, was determined to excel with perfection and was always functioning in overdrive. But her solo efforts left her team feeling sidelined, and the stress of carrying everything alone drained her energy.

Spark Moment:

After a particularly overwhelming week, Sarah overheard two of her team members discussing how they felt out of the loop. Realizing she was unintentionally isolating them, she decided to change her approach.

Path to Thrive:

Sarah started involving her team in brainstorming sessions and gradually let them take the lead on portions of projects. The results weren't always perfect, and some ideas flopped, but overall, morale improved, and collaboration strengthened. The team felt valued, and Sarah no longer carried everything alone.

Time to Shine:

Sarah discovered that leadership isn't about proving you can do it all—it's about bringing people together to create something better than you could alone. Letting go of control was tough, but over time, it built trust, engagement, and real results.

Case Study 2: When Less Is Actually More

Stage Setting:

Allison, a new sales rep, believed that dazzling clients with extravagant meetings and big promises was the key to success. But despite her efforts, deals kept slipping through her fingers.

Spark Moment:

After a series of failed pitches, a client candidly told her, "I like your enthusiasm, but I need a partner I can count on, not someone selling me the big ideas." The feedback stung, but it made her rethink her entire approach.

Path to Thrive:

Working with her manager, Allison stripped down her pitches to the essentials: reliable solutions, clear expectations, and honest conversations. She didn't win over every account, but she built stronger relationships with the ones who valued her style.

Time to Shine:

Allison learned that trust is built through consistency, not theatrics. It wasn't about making the biggest impression—it was about showing up, following through, and delivering value.

Case Study 3: Engaging Beyond the Comfort Zone

Stage Setting:
Brooke was one of the least experienced members in a high-energy marketing team where quick thinking and confidence were the norm. She felt out of place and defaulted to staying quiet, convincing herself it was better to observe until she was completely sure of her ideas. But the longer she stayed silent, the more invisible she became.

Spark Moment:
During a tense client meeting, the team struggled to land on a solution. Brooke saw a clear way forward but hesitated—until a teammate voiced the exact same idea and received praise. Seeing someone else get credit for what she had kept to herself was a wake-up call: her ideas had value, but they meant nothing if she didn't speak up.

Path to Thrive:
Determined to change, Brooke set a goal: speak up at least once in every meeting, even if she wasn't 100% confident. Some contributions landed well, others didn't, but she kept at it. Over time, she got in the habit of voicing her input, and she built a reputation for solid insights.

Time to Shine:
Brooke learned that waiting for perfection meant missing opportunities. Confidence wasn't about always being right; it was about contributing and learning from the process. By stepping up, she became a valued presence in the room instead of just an observer.

Quick note:

Create a Work Journal to capture your ideas, insights, and progress along your journey. Whether it's a physical notebook, your phone's notes app, or an online journal, choose something comfortable and convenient. No rules here—just go with what you'll enjoy and use consistently.

Now that you've explored what it means to show up as your real self, here's how to keep that momentum going in your daily work life.

Reflection Checkpoints

1. True to You Check-In

Ego loves to take control—it can push you to perform or push you to the shadows. Checking in with yourself regularly helps you notice when ego slips into the driver's seat. Staying self-aware is what empowers you to step back into alignment with your authentic self.

Something to Try:

Reflect briefly whenever you sense you've drifted from your true self at work. In your Work Journal, consider:

- Did I feel the urge to impress, perform, or compete instead of just being genuine?
- Was there a moment I chose silence over speaking up—and why?
- How would the authentic me handle similar moments differently next time?

No pressure, just note your honest reflection that helps you stay true.

2. Stay in Sync Tracker

Consistent, authentic actions build trust and credibility. Small, genuine acts of reliability add up quickly, helping others see you as dependable and sincere.

Something to Try:

Identify three simple actions that reflect who you genuinely are and align naturally with your values. These might include things like thoughtfully acknowledging colleagues, giving clear updates, or proactively checking in on teammates. Note these actions in your Work Journal, and when inspired, write down insights like:

- How does acting consistently in alignment with my values make me feel?
- Am I noticing positive responses or stronger connections from others?

Track lightly; learn deeply.

3. Shine Prompt

Small, intentional actions showcase your authentic self. Over time, these tiny moments build your confidence, spark genuine connections, and inspire authenticity around you.

Something to Try:

Choose one simple action—something authentic to you—that allows you to shine naturally. Examples might be clarifying something unclear, thoughtfully offering your perspective, or lending spontaneous help to someone in need. Whenever you practice your daily shine, reflect briefly (mentally or in your journal):

- Did it boost my confidence or bring a sense of ease?
- Did it encourage authenticity around me?

Small, genuine acts matter more than you think.

Psssst... Over Here

Feeling unsure? That means you're growing. Let it be messy. Keep going. The shine shows up when you do.

Last Call Spark

Showing up fully doesn't require a spotlight or a grand entrance—it's about consistency, presence, and being real even when no one's watching. When you bring your whole self to the table, you build trust, make waves in all the right ways, and lay the runway for takeoff. Authenticity is your boarding pass.

Chapter 2

To Your Own Self Be True: Cultivate Self-Awareness to Bring Your Best to Work

What if work didn't feel like putting on a costume? Too often, we feel pressure to mold ourselves into a "work version" that's more polished, more neutral, or more palatable. But the professionals who make the biggest impact aren't chameleons—they're people who lean into what makes them unique. Your interests, background, and quirks? They're assets, not distractions. Imagine if your creativity from photography helped shape presentations or your soccer experience gave you an edge in teamwork. This chapter examines how bringing your full self to work can be a strength, not a risk.

Confessions of a Showboater

In the early days of my career, I was determined to dazzle. If I wasn't delivering the most polished ideas, the most detailed analysis, or the most memorable presentations, I felt like I was falling short. I wasn't just doing my job—I was curating a show.

The irony? All that effort to impress meant I was missing the real work. I was so caught up in making things look extraordinary that I lost sight of what was most important and lost touch with my genuine style. I eventually realized that success isn't about putting on an act; it's about showing up, engaging in the work, and making meaningful contributions beyond the surface.

Why Knowing Yourself is Your Career Advantage

★ **Authenticity is Easier Than Playing a Role**
Trying to be someone you're not is exhausting. Owning your strengths and values makes it easier to show up with confidence and consistency.

★ **Self-Awareness Leads to Smarter Choices**
Understanding what energizes you—and what drains you—helps you navigate opportunities, roles, and challenges more effectively.

★ **Confidence Comes from Clarity**

When you know who you are and what you stand for, decision-making becomes less about seeking approval and more about staying true to yourself.

★ **Your Unique Perspective is Your Strength**

Instead of trying to fit in, bring your individuality to the table. The workplace thrives on diverse voices, and yours is needed.

★ **The More You Own Your Story, the More Others Respect It**

People respond to authenticity. The more self-aware you are, the more trust and credibility you build with those around you.

My Own Lesson: Showing Up with Purpose, Not Perfection

I had the chance to lead a major proposal—a "big break" moment when I'd present directly to our Chief Operating Officer. Determined to impress, I overprepared. Late nights, endless refinements, and layers of extra detail, a 15-slide deck—I was going to kill it!

Then, during a practice run, my manager stopped me mid-way and said, "This is going on too long for the COO to absorb. If you could pitch just one thing, what would it be?" I screeched to a halt. I had been so focused on showing off my work that I'd completely lost focus. My approach had turned into a performance instead of something meaningful.

I scrapped the fluff and homed in on one clear, impactful idea. When I presented, it was simple and sharp. The COO immediately saw the value and gave his support. I walked away with success, not because I had "dazzled" anyone, but because I finally showed up in the way that counted: on point, engaged, and aligned with what truly mattered.

The Lesson Earned

I used to think showing up meant doing *more*: more detail, more polish, more effort to show I was ready. But that day, standing in front of the COO, I realized that showing up isn't about adding stuff. It's about clarity. It's about knowing what matters and making sure *that* is heard.

I prepped for that meeting convinced that my endless preparation would impress. I walked out of it understanding that my real job was to strip away the excess and let the *right* things shine. I didn't need to overcompensate—I just needed to be present, engaged, and confident in what I was bringing to the table.

And honestly? That lesson has stuck with me far more than the actual outcome of that presentation.

Case Study 1: When Authenticity Needs a Filter

Stage Setting:
Claudia was known for her vibrant personality and loved bringing fun into the workplace. As a new administrative assistant at a boutique investment firm, she wanted to make an impression. When she learned it was her boss's birthday, she decided to surprise him with a playful Marilyn Monroe-style serenade—blonde wig and all.

Spark Moment:
While the gesture got laughs, Claudia quickly realized she had misread the company culture. Her boss was polite but visibly uncomfortable, and whispers spread about whether her approach was appropriate for the workplace. She hadn't considered how her fun style might land in a professional setting.

Path to Thrive:
Instead of letting embarrassment define her, Claudia adjusted how she expressed her personality at work. She brought energy in more subtle ways—organizing events, adding humor in meetings, and building relationships without crossing professional boundaries. However, it took time to rebuild her professional reputation, and some colleagues still saw her as too informal.

Time to Shine:
Claudia learned that authenticity shines brightest when it's adapted to the environment. While she found her footing, she also realized that some first impressions take longer to change. Being true to herself didn't mean ignoring the realities of workplace culture.

Case Study 2: The Fine Line Between Sharing and Oversharing

Stage Setting:
Helen, a new contract manager, wanted to connect with her team and prove she belonged in a high-pressure corporate environment. To build camaraderie, she openly discussed challenges, often venting about frustrations and self-doubt. She hoped her honesty would make her more relatable.

Spark Moment:
One day, after sharing her struggles in a meeting, Helen noticed an awkward shift in the room. Instead of engaging, colleagues seemed hesitant, unsure how to respond. A peer later advised her that while openness was good, too much personal sharing could make her seem less confident and capable.

Path to Thrive:
Taking the feedback to heart, Helen adjusted her approach. Instead of venting, she reframed challenges as learning experiences and focused on how she was improving. While this helped her gain

back some credibility, some colleagues still viewed her as uncertain in her role, and she had to work harder to prove her expertise.

Time to Shine:
Helen discovered that vulnerability is powerful when paired with professionalism. However, she also learned that first impressions can linger, and not every mistake can be undone quickly. Balancing openness with self-assurance became an ongoing challenge, rather than an immediate fix.

Case Study 3: The Identity Tug-of-War

Stage Setting:
Maya, a young product manager, prided herself on being a straight shooter. She believed blunt honesty was key to effective work, but her feedback often left meetings in awkward silence. Over time, she noticed colleagues hesitated to loop her into discussions, making her feel sidelined and unheard.

Spark Moment:
After a tense project review where she flatly dismissed an idea, a teammate later told her that while her insights were valuable, her delivery made people shut down. Maya had assumed her directness was a strength, but now she wondered if it was holding her back instead of setting her apart.

Path to Thrive:
Determined to adapt without losing her authenticity, she refined her approach, asking sharp but constructive questions instead of immediately shutting ideas down. Instead of saying, *"This won't work,"* she framed discussions around what needed to be fixed or improved.

At first, the shift felt small, but she soon noticed a change: her colleagues started seeking her opinion rather than avoiding it.

Time to Shine:
Maya realized that self-awareness isn't about losing who you are. It's about understanding your impact. She was still honest, still direct—but now, she was also learning how to be more effective.

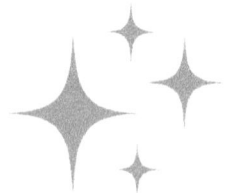

Let's turn that self-awareness into action with a few ways to keep your values and voice front and center.

1. True to You Check-In

Think of your core values as your personal GPS—they're there to keep you on track when work starts feeling like rush-hour traffic. Staying aligned with your values helps you navigate confidently, even through tricky turns.

Something to Try:

Quickly replay a recent work moment that felt off-course or uncomfortable, then ask yourself:

- Which of my core values got bumped out of the driver's seat?
- Was there pressure or fear pulling me in a different direction?
- What's one easy adjustment that'll get my internal GPS back online?

Just a quick tune-up—no overhaul required.

2. Stay in Sync Tracker

Authenticity at work isn't about spilling everything—it's about adding the right spice to the dish. Knowing when, where, and how much of your true personality to sprinkle in makes your professional interactions more flavorful without overwhelming the recipe.

Something to Try:

After interactions that mattered, take a mental taste test:

- Was my "seasoning" just right for the audience and setting?
- Did I overshare, undershare, or hit that Goldilocks zone?
- What tiny tweak will enhance my professional "recipe" next time?

Make it playful—a dash here, a pinch there—to find your perfect blend.

3. Shine Prompt

Showing up authentically is contagious (in the best way!). Every time you share a real, genuine piece of yourself, you help build an environment where your teammates feel comfortable being real, too.

Something to Try :

Pick one small-but-mighty part of yourself (your humor, curiosity, empathy, or sharp eye for detail) and intentionally let it shine today. Later, quickly reflect:

- Did my mini-moment of authenticity spark connection or bring out smiles?
- Did it make my own day brighter or boost my courage to keep showing up as me?

Think of it as dropping little sparks of authenticity and watching them glow.

Dear *Younger Me...*

Hey there, Little Julee. You weren't behind.
You were growing through it.
Mistakes were simply your dues being paid.
It's all good. Don't white knuckle it.

Last Call Spark

There's only one you—and that's your superpower. When you stop editing yourself to fit the room and start honoring what makes you you, things shift. You connect deeper, lead stronger, and feel way more at home in your own skin. Authenticity isn't just a vibe—it's your secret sauce.

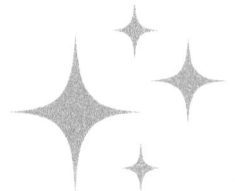

Chapter 3:

Leave Negative Energy Behind: Shed Limiting Beliefs and Embrace Your Full Potential

Ever had a thought that whispered, *you're not good enough*? Or caught yourself comparing your progress to someone else's highlight reel? These mental blocks can quietly chip away at confidence and momentum. But here's the truth: negative energy—whether self-doubt, comparison, or resentment—holds you back more than any external challenge ever could. The good news? You can train your mind to work for you instead of against you. In this chapter, we'll unpack how to recognize and release the limiting beliefs that are draining your energy and keeping you stuck.

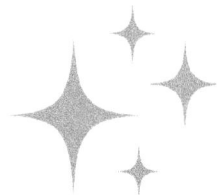

Confessions of a Winzilla

Outwardly, I was all smiles, the ultimate team player. Inside, I was laser-focused on winning. I needed to prove myself, to climb the ranks, to outshine everyone else. My ambition wasn't just a motivator—it was an obsession.

I had a crazy drive to dominate the game. I wanted to be the best, the first, the most recognized. But that tunnel vision came at a cost. The wins that mattered most weren't the ones I racked up alone, but the ones built on something bigger than just personal achievement. Collaboration and real impact trump empty victories.

Why Mindset Matters More Than You Think

- **Your Thoughts Shape Your Outcomes**

  Negative thinking creates invisible barriers. Reframing setbacks as lessons transforms obstacles into stepping stones.

- **Doubt is Normal—But It Shouldn't Be in the Driver's Seat**

  Feeling uncertain is part of growth. The key is not letting self-doubt hold you back from taking action.

- **Positivity Fuels Progress**
  A growth-oriented mindset helps you stay open to opportunities, even when things don't go as planned.

- **Letting Go of Perfection Opens More Doors**
  Perfectionism slows you down. Striving for progress over perfection makes you more adaptable and successful.

- **Your Energy is Contagious—Make It Count**
  The way you show up affects those around you. Being solution-focused and optimistic makes you someone others want to work with.

My Own Lesson: When Winning Almost Led Me to Losing

In a team meeting, an exciting new project was up for grabs. The conversation naturally leaned toward a colleague taking the lead. But instead of letting things unfold, I jumped in and volunteered myself.

The room fell into an awkward silence before I was granted the role. My colleague's reaction? Cold. Over the next few meetings, she barely made eye contact and kept her responses clipped.

Eventually, I asked what was wrong. Her answer? "That was a tacky move."

My first instinct? Defensiveness. But deep down, I knew she was right. I had pushed myself forward—not because I was the best fit, but because I was driven by insecurity and competition. And now, our project was at risk.

The next day, I did something uncomfortable: I apologized, then asked if we could co-lead, recognizing that the project needed both of us. That shift didn't make us best friends, but it restored some mutual respect and helped set the project up for success.

The Lesson Earned

That moment, when my colleague looked me in the eye and called my move *tacky*—oof. It stung. Not because it was harsh, but because she wasn't wrong.

I had grabbed at an opportunity out of *fear*. Fear that if I didn't push, I'd be left behind. But that fear-driven move? It didn't feel like a win at all. It felt uncomfortable. And for good reason.

What I learned that day wasn't just about being a better teammate. It was about trust. Trusting that my work would speak for itself. Trusting that I didn't need to shove my way in to be recognized. Trusting that success doesn't have to feel like stepping on someone else's toes.

I still cringe when I think about that moment. But I also carry the lesson with me: There's a difference between going after what you want and forcing it. And if it *feels* wrong, there's usually a reason.

Case Study 1: Breaking Up with Imposter Syndrome

Stage Setting:
Rina was thrilled to land her first product manager role, but being surrounded by experienced colleagues made her feel like she didn't belong. She held back in meetings, second-guessed herself, and feared someone would expose her as not qualified enough. Her excitement quickly turned into self-doubt.

Spark Moment:
During a project presentation, Rina made a minor mistake and braced for criticism. Instead, her manager simply corrected the issue and moved on. She realized she was the only one making a big deal out of her imperfections.

Path to Thrive:
Determined to change, Rina started asking

more questions, speaking up, and owning her contributions. Not everything landed perfectly, but she saw that growth came from engagement, not silence.

Time to Shine:
Rina learned that imposter syndrome thrives in isolation. The more she leaned in, the more she saw that competence isn't about knowing everything—it's about learning, adapting, and contributing.

Case Study 2: From Competitor to Collaborator

Stage Setting:
Lily had always been driven, thriving on being the best. But in her marketing role, she treated every project as a competition, constantly trying to outshine her teammates. She thought ambition was her strength—until she realized she was being left out of key conversations.

Spark Moment:
In a brainstorming session, she dismissed a colleague's idea, only to watch the team rally behind it. That's when she realized she wasn't elevating the work—she was shutting down ideas that weren't her own.

Path to Thrive:
Lily made a conscious effort to amplify her teammates' ideas instead of dominating conversations. It wasn't

easy, and at first, it felt unnatural. She still had moments when she wanted to compete, but as she began supporting others, she saw her own ideas gain more traction. Trust within the team grew, though shifting perceptions took longer than she expected.

Time to Shine:
Lily learned that true leadership isn't about being the best in the room—it's about bringing out the best in the team. While she still had ambition, she realized that success wasn't just about personal wins—it was about collective growth. However, she also saw that not everyone quickly embraced her new approach, and she had to prove herself over time.

Case Study 3: Breaking Free from the Fear of Failure

Stage Setting:
Nina was known for her flawless execution but only within her comfort zone. Whenever a leadership opportunity came up, she let someone else take it. She wasn't lacking ability—she was afraid of failing. Playing it safe made her reliable, but not promotable.

Spark Moment:
When a major project needed a lead, she stepped back—until she saw someone else take it on, struggle, and ultimately succeed by figuring things out along the way. That's when she realized it wasn't about perfection—it was about showing up.

Path to Thrive:
Nina took the next opportunity that came her way. She made mistakes, and some setbacks shook her confidence. But instead of retreating, she leaned into the discomfort and kept going. While her first project didn't go perfectly, she proved to herself that she was capable of handling more responsibility. Some of her colleagues still saw her as hesitant, and earning their confidence took longer than she expected.

Time to Shine:
Nina learned that growth is about learning from failure, not running away from it. Confidence isn't built overnight, and fear doesn't disappear instantly. It fades with repeated action. Playing it safe had kept her stagnant; stepping up set her on a new path, even if setbacks still surfaced along the way.

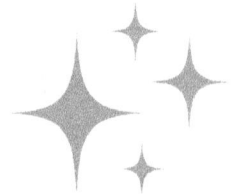

Ready to let go of the noise and step into your full potential? These checkpoints will help you track what's worth carrying—and what's not.

1. True to You Check-In

Limiting beliefs often lurk quietly beneath the surface, holding you back without you realizing it. Once you uncover these hidden roadblocks, you can rewrite them into empowering stories that reflect who you really are.

Something to Try:

Reflect briefly on recent experiences where you may have felt stuck or hesitant:

- What limiting belief was quietly influencing my thoughts or decisions?
- How can I rewrite this negative story into one that empowers and encourages me?
- What's one tiny action step I could take to shift this belief?

Short reflections in your journal help you break through internal barriers and own your full potential.

2. Stay in Sync Tracker

Negativity doesn't just live inside your head—it sometimes slips into your interactions, shaping how you show up to others. Catching these external moments of negativity or judgment helps you consciously choose a more authentic, positive presence.

Something to Try:

After notable interactions, quickly ask yourself:

- Did negativity, judgment, or competitiveness show up externally (in words, tone, or reactions)?
- What simple reminder can help me show up with more genuine positivity next time?

Brief notes or mental check-ins are enough to shift toward authenticity and positivity in your interactions.

3. Shine Prompt

Small, intentional positivity acts like mental sunshine, gradually brightening your outlook and strengthening your confidence.

Something to Try:

Each day, choose one small, intentional action to spark positivity—like giving genuine praise, practicing patience, or calmly speaking up. Quickly reflect at day's end:

- How did this small action affect my mindset or interactions today?
- Did it help replace negativity with a feeling of connection, courage, or calm?

Small, consistent steps build lasting positivity.

Last Call Spark

Shed the weight, ditch the drama, and step into the lighter, brighter version of yourself. Letting go of the stories and energy that hold you back makes room for confidence, creativity, and (gasp) even joy. Whenever possible, choose progress over pressure.

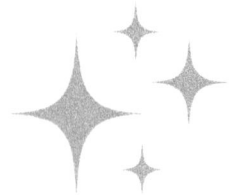

Chapter 4

Authenticity is Your Compass: Let Your True Self Guide the Road You Want to Travel

You've probably heard it before: *Be authentic*! But what does that look like when building a career? It's easy to get lost in the noise (advice from mentors, industry trends, social media comparisons, etc.). But here's the reality: only you know what truly aligns with your values, strengths, and aspirations. This chapter isn't about making one "right" decision. It's about learning to trust yourself enough to navigate twists, turns, and unexpected detours with confidence. Let's look at ways to block out external pressure and chart a course that feels genuinely right for you.

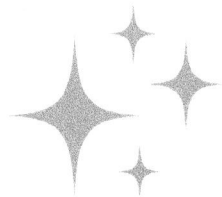

Confessions of a Career Conformist

I was the poster child for playing it safe. Follow the rules, chase the titles, climb the corporate ladder: check, check, check. It felt good to know I was "on track."

But here's the thing: Just because something looks good on paper doesn't mean it feels right in your gut. I was so focused on what I should be doing that I never asked myself what I wanted to be doing. When I finally did? That's when my real career began.

Why Your Path Matters More Than Others' Expectations

- **Success Feels Better When It's Truly Yours**

  Following someone else's blueprint might seem safe, but true fulfillment comes from carving a path that aligns with your values and goals.

- **Authenticity Attracts the Right Opportunities**

  The more you stay true to what excites you, the more likely you are to draw in the roles, connections, and experiences that genuinely fit.

★ **You're the Expert on What Works for You**
No one else has lived your experiences, faced your challenges, or seen the world through your lens. Own your perspective—it's an asset.

★ **Taking Risks Builds Confidence**
Every time you make a decision based on what feels right for you, not based on what others say, you strengthen your ability to trust yourself.

★ **A Unique Path Leads to Unique Success**
The careers that stand out are the ones shaped by personal choices, unexpected pivots, and bold moves. Make your journey one worth telling.

My Own Lesson: Listening to My Instincts, Not My Logic

On paper, my career was perfect: working at a prestigious VC firm in Manhattan, fast-tracking toward success. But behind the scenes? I was exhausted, burned out, and suffocated by the relentless pace.

So, I made a bold move: I quit, packed up, and relocated to San Francisco to reset.

I casually posted my resume online, thinking hey, you never know. A week later, a recruiter called about an executive assistant role at an enterprise software company. My first thought? *Hard pass*. Lower title, lower pay, wrong industry. But I agreed to interview, just for practice.

One interview turned into two, then three. Then they made an offer, saying, "We know you're overqualified, but there is upward potential, and we'd really love you on the team."

Logically, I should have said no. But something in my gut told me otherwise. Despite the doubts swirling in my head, I accepted.

That "bad choice on paper" became one of the best decisions of my career. I stayed 13 years, growing into leadership roles that shaped my entire professional path.

The Lesson Earned

On paper, going from a high-powered career in Manhattan for a lower-paying assistant job in an industry I knew nothing about was *stupid*. Absolutely, unequivocally stupid.

And yet.

That so-called "wrong move" turned into one of the best decisions of my life. It taught me that logic doesn't always hold the answers, that instincts *matter*. Sometimes the thing that *feels* right—even if it makes no sense—ends up being exactly what you needed.

I could have ignored that gut feeling and held out for something that looked better on a resume. But then, I would have missed the job that gave me a 13-year runway to build the career I have now.

I guess the lesson is this: Sometimes, your gut knows where you're going before your head does. Listen to it.

Case Study 1: The 'Wrong' Move That Led to the Right Path

Stage Setting:
Maria had spent years excelling in corporate finance, building a solid career with an impressive salary and clear advancement opportunities. Yet, despite checking every career milestone, she felt detached from her work. She craved creativity and purpose but worried about throwing away years of effort for something uncertain.

Spark Moment:
An unexpected nonprofit leadership opportunity

landed in her inbox. It lacked the prestige of her current role but aligned deeply with her values. She hesitated, torn between playing it safe or making a bold change. Then, she realized that staying put out of fear meant ignoring the instincts that had fueled her success in the first place.

Path to Thrive:
Despite initial doubts, Maria took the leap. The transition was tough—she had to navigate a steep learning curve and adjust to a different work environment. Some colleagues questioned why she left a prestigious role, and moments of self-doubt crept in. She missed aspects of her old job, and progress in her new role was slower than she had hoped.

Time to Shine:
Maria discovered that success isn't just about climbing higher; it's about climbing in the right direction. Though her new career path was rewarding, she had to accept that change came with trade-offs. Some parts of her transition were fulfilling, while others required ongoing adjustment.

Case Study 2: The Clash Between Fitting In and Standing Out

Stage Setting:
Evelyn had just started her first job at a well-established corporate firm. She observed her

colleagues and quickly realized that the workplace had a distinct, formal culture. Her usual upbeat, casual style felt out of place, and she found herself adapting: dressing differently, toning down her humor, and mirroring how others spoke in meetings. Over time, she began to wonder: Was she blending in too much?

Spark Moment:
During a team meeting, a senior manager presented a creative problem-solving challenge. Evelyn, who had a fresh perspective, had an idea but hesitated. Was it too informal? Too unconventional? She stayed silent. Later, a colleague shared a similar idea, and it was met with enthusiasm. That moment was an epiphany: she had something valuable to offer, but she had held back in an effort to "fit in."

Path to Thrive:
Determined to find balance, Evelyn started testing ways to bring more of herself into work. She contributed in meetings when she had ideas, shared small bits of her humor in one-on-one conversations, and gradually let her personality shine without disregarding the professional culture. Some efforts landed well, others didn't, but she was finding a way to be herself without feeling like an outsider.

Time to Shine:
Evelyn realized that authenticity isn't all or nothing—it's about knowing when and how to bring your true

self forward. She didn't need to change who she was, but she also didn't need to rebel against the office culture. Over time, she found confidence in balancing both.

Case Study 3: The Shiny Opportunity That Wasn't the Right Fit

Stage Setting:
Jordan had always believed that saying yes to every opportunity was the key to success. When she was offered an internal move to a prestigious, high-profile team, she jumped at the chance, not fully understanding what the role entailed. The title sounded impressive, and she assumed she would love it. But as the months passed, she realized that the work didn't align with her strengths, and she struggled to stay engaged.

Spark Moment:
A few months in, Jordan noticed something unsettling: she no longer felt excited about work. Tasks that once energized her now felt like a burden, and she dreaded meetings. It wasn't just a learning curve; it was a fundamental misalignment. She had chased prestige instead of considering what truly motivated her.

Path to Thrive:
Rather than forcing herself to love the role, Jordan reflected on what she liked about her work. She

spoke with her manager and explored alternative opportunities within the company. She had to admit that not every opportunity is the right one, and stepping back to recalibrate wasn't failure. It was learning.

Time to Shine:
Jordan realized that success isn't about taking every opportunity—it's about taking the right ones. Saying no (or stepping back) was just as important as saying yes. The experience wasn't wasted; it gave her clarity about the work that fulfilled her, and that was a lesson worth learning early in her career.

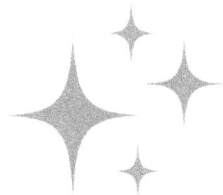

Your path won't look like anyone else's, and that's the point. Let's reflect on how to keep making decisions that are true to you.

1. True to You Check-In

Early in your career, you might not always have full control over your role or responsibilities—and that's totally okay. Even within limits, there's room to explore choices and actions that genuinely resonate with your goals.

Something to Try:

Reflect briefly on a recent work situation or task:

- Within the expectations set for me, did I find small ways to align with my own career goals or interests?
- Was there a moment I felt pulled away from my personal direction by external pressure or expectations?
- What's one manageable, realistic step I can take next time to stay closer to what feels true to me, even within my current responsibilities?

Simple notes in your journal help you keep sight of your goals, even when navigating constraints.

2. Stay in Sync Tracker

Sometimes, career growth means adapting to tasks you didn't necessarily choose. Recognizing how well you handle these situations builds confidence and resilience, preparing you to guide your path more clearly over time.

Something to Try:

When facing tasks or assignments you wouldn't necessarily pick for yourself, quickly reflect:

- How did I adapt or pivot within these assigned responsibilities?
- Did I learn something new or surprising by working through something I didn't initially choose?
- Can I appreciate my ability to flexibly navigate assignments, even when they aren't my first choice?

Brief check-ins remind you that career growth often comes from unexpected places.

3. Shine Prompt

Even small decisions can build confidence in your own judgment. While you might not control everything at work, your inner voice still matters—and practicing listening to it will serve you long term.

Something to Try:

Choose one small work-related action today (like suggesting a minor improvement, sharing your perspective in a discussion, or asking a clarifying question). Trust your own judgment fully, even if it feels minor. Reflect briefly afterward:

- How did it feel to trust myself in a small, manageable moment?
- Did this boost my confidence or help clarify what I might want more of in my future career?

Small, consistent steps help your inner guidance become stronger over time.

Reminder *to Mind Yourself*

FOMO? Grass over there looking pretty green? Everyone else's path looks great from the outside. Stick with yours. Your behind-the-scenes work is where the growth happens.

Last Call Spark

Spoiler: there's no "right" way to build your career, but there is a way that's right for you. When you trust your gut, embrace the detours, and let go of everyone else's map, that's when things get good. Your path doesn't need to look perfect, especially since there is no such thing as perfect. It just needs to feel like it's yours.

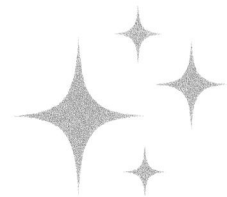

Thrive and SHINE

H

Harness Your Strengths

You've explored how to show up authentically. Now, let's build on that by sharpening your strengths and stepping into your power. In this section, we're moving beyond *who you are* and focusing on *what you bring to the table*: your skills, instincts, and the unique toolkit that makes you valuable.

For early-stage professionals, this can feel tricky. There's often an unspoken pressure to "earn" the right to speak up. But the truth? Your instincts are already valuable. The key is learning how to back them up with confidence and proof. When you combine intuition with facts, you elevate both your credibility and your influence.

This section is about refining your strengths—not changing who you are but learning how to own what makes you great and amplify it with the right tools. We'll cover how to trust your gut while sharpening your logic, set boundaries while staying engaged, and build resilience without burning out.

Strength isn't about taking up space just to be seen. It's about showing up with clarity, conviction, and the ability to create real impact. Let's get to work.

Chapter 5

Trust Your Instincts, Validate with Proof: Combine Intuition with Facts for Confident Decision-Making

You've got a gut feeling about a decision, but how do you make sure it holds weight? Intuition is powerful, but when paired with tangible proof, it becomes your superpower. We are often encouraged to second-guess ourselves, but real confidence comes from trusting your instincts while also backing them up with research, data, and lived experience. In this chapter, we'll break down how to sharpen your instincts and validate them with concrete evidence, so you can make decisions with clarity and conviction.

Confessions of an Improv Artist

Early on, I relied on quick thinking and adaptability. In school, last-minute cramming worked just fine, and in my early career, I leaned on instincts to get by. I figured preparation was overrated. Why spend hours rehearsing when I could just adapt in the moment?

For a while, this worked. But the higher the stakes got, the more I realized that *improvising isn't the same as being prepared*. My quick thinking could only take me so far. At some point, I overcorrected, shifting to the opposite extreme, over-planning and overpreparing to avoid any risk of failure. Eventually, I found balance: preparation gives you a foundation, but adaptability is still key to handling the unexpected.

Why Instinct + Evidence is Your Ultimate Power Move

- **Your Gut is Smarter Than You Think**
  Instinct isn't magic—it's built from experience, observation, and subtle cues your brain processes before you're even aware of them.

- **Facts Make Your Intuition Stronger**
  A gut feeling backed by data is an unstoppable

combination. Trust your instincts, but verify them with research, feedback, or past trends.

★ **Confidence Comes from Knowing, Not Guessing**

The strongest leaders don't rely on hunches alone. They gather insights, ask questions, and then make informed, bold decisions.

★ **Mistakes Are Just Part of Refining Your Judgment**

No one gets it right 100% of the time. Every wrong turn sharpens your ability to recognize the right one next time.

★ **Trusting Yourself Encourages Others to Trust You**

People respect decisiveness. The more you practice balancing instinct with proof, the more credibility you'll build.

My Own Lesson: Data, Diligence, and a Slice of Humble Pie

I had built a strong reputation leading Learning & Development programs, earning positive feedback from executives, until I met the Head of Finance for Europe. He was skeptical, direct, and unimpressed with my ideas. He didn't care about feel-good feedback. He wanted proof.

When I met him in person during a training session in England, he hit me with tough, data-driven questions that I wasn't fully prepared to answer. I had relied on instincts and qualitative feedback, but that wasn't enough. Shortly after, he sent my boss a critical note questioning the program's (and my) effectiveness. Ouch.

I had a choice: resent his skepticism or rise to meet it. With coaching from my boss, I committed to building a stronger foundation of proof. I doubled down on data, improved my analysis, and backed up my work with real metrics. Over time, the same executive who once dismissed me started trusting my insights. And the day he sent an email with a smiley face? I knew I had turned a critic into a supporter.

The Lesson Earned

I used to think my actions alone were enough to prove my value. But actions without evidence? That's just a strong opinion.

Instead of seeing skepticism as criticism, I learned to see it as an invitation to level up. Hard data didn't take away from my creativity—it made my ideas stronger, sharper, and more persuasive.

Now, I don't only trust my gut; I validate it. And that's what turns confidence into credibility.

Case Study 1: The Gut Feeling That Needed a Green Light

Stage Setting

Gillian, a junior account executive at a PR agency, was helping develop a product launch campaign for a lifestyle brand. The senior strategists favored a traditional influencer approach, but Gillian had a gut feeling that user-generated content (UGC) would resonate more. The product appealed to younger consumers who engaged heavily with social media, and she instinctively felt that giving them a role in the campaign would drive more organic buzz.

Spark Moment

While she believed in her idea, Gillian hesitated. She was the newest staff in the room, and the senior team had already aligned with a direction. Instead of pushing her idea impulsively, she took a step back. That night, she researched UGC success stories, found engagement data, and even did a quick analysis of competitor campaigns.

Path to Thrive

With her research in hand, Gillian asked her manager

for input, positioning it as a question rather than a challenge: "I noticed that brands using user-generated content see a big engagement lift. Do you think there's room for us to incorporate that?" Her manager was intrigued but noncommittal, so she kept gathering insights. She tested a small-scale version by posting a customer participation prompt on the brand's social media and tracking engagement. When the results were promising, she brought them to her team.

Time to Shine
The campaign wasn't overhauled, but her insights led to some last-minute adjustments. The team integrated UGC into the campaign as a secondary component, and the results were positive. It wasn't a dramatic win, but it was a step forward. More importantly, Gillian learned that backing up her instincts with proof made people take her seriously, even when she didn't have the loudest voice in the room.

Case Study 2: When a Hunch Became a Mismatch

Stage Setting
Tori, a customer experience specialist at a fast-growing software company, had built a reputation for understanding user needs. She often spotted small adjustments that improved customer satisfaction,

which made her confident in her instincts. When she was asked to lead a virtual training on a new product update, she saw it as her chance to shine.

Spark Moment

Tori had a gut feeling that one particular feature—one she personally loved—would be a hit with users. Instead of checking recent customer feedback or consulting the product team, she designed her session around this assumption. She figured her experience with customers had given her a strong sense of what they needed, and she didn't want to waste time second-guessing herself.

Path to Thrive

The session flopped. Attendees barely reacted to the feature she highlighted, and most of the questions focused on a different area, one she had brushed over. In the debrief, her manager gave her direct but constructive feedback: "Your instincts are great, but you missed a big opportunity by not validating them." Checking user survey data would have revealed that customers had more pressing concerns elsewhere.

Time to Shine

Tori was embarrassed but took it as a learning moment. Instead of sulking, she asked her manager how she could better prepare next time. She started to make a habit of gut-checking her instincts with real data. A few months later, she led another training—this time after doing thorough research—and the engagement was noticeably stronger. The experience stung, but it taught her a lasting lesson: intuition is powerful, but without validation, it can steer you in the wrong direction.

Case Study 3: Fast, But Not So Furious – Learning to Pause Before Pouncing

Stage Setting

Leanne, an operations analyst at a fast-growing startup, prided herself on being quick on her feet. She was in charge of pulling key performance data for leadership meetings, and she had built a reputation for being sharp and efficient.

Spark Moment

One morning, her manager messaged her in a panic: they needed updated revenue projections before an executive call in 30 minutes. Leanne had pulled similar numbers before, so she trusted her instincts, made quick calculations, and sent over the report—without double-checking her formulas.

Path to Thrive

Minutes after sending it, Leanne's stomach dropped. She spotted an error—she had overlooked an adjustment in the revenue model, and her numbers were off. It wasn't catastrophic, but it was enough to cause confusion in the meeting. When her manager circled back, she gave Leanne some direct feedback: "You were right to move fast, but rushing without verifying hurt us. Next time, take a minute to check before sending something to be presented."

Time to Shine

Leanne was frustrated with herself, but she had to move on. She implemented a simple rule: pause and verify. Instead of pushing under pressure, she built a habit of taking one full minute to review her work before hitting send. She learned that speed and output are valuable, but when the stakes are high, a second look can make all the difference.

Here's how to strengthen your decision-making with a blend of gut feel and grounded evidence.

1. True to You Check-In

Your gut instinct sparks ideas, but combining it with evidence is like giving your vision HD clarity: suddenly, others can see exactly what you see. Blending intuition with facts amplifies your impact and helps your ideas resonate clearly with others.

Something to Try:

Briefly reflect on a recent decision or recommendation:

- Did I lean mostly on gut instinct or back it up clearly with evidence?
- Could one clear fact or concrete example have clarified my idea further for my audience?
- How can I use this balanced approach next time to ensure my ideas land clearly and powerfully?

Quick notes sharpen your insight.

2. Stay in Sync Tracker

Being prepared isn't just about you; it's about how others perceive your credibility and professionalism. Thoughtful preparation signals to your team that you're reliable, trustworthy, and ready to handle important moments gracefully.

Something to Try:

After meaningful interactions (meetings, presentations, or critical conversations), pause briefly:

- Which specific points or evidence helped others trust my input or feel confident in my approach?
- Did my preparation help create a sense of calm or clarity for myself and others?
- Could adjusting the depth of my preparation next time further enhance my effectiveness?

Brief reflections keep your professional presence polished.

3. Shine Prompt

Gathering evidence consistently grounds your creative instincts, steadily increasing your confidence and sharpening your communication. Over time, small daily habits turn great ideas into trusted, powerful insights.

Something to Try:

Choose one idea or decision you're working on, and intentionally find one simple piece of supporting evidence (a quick fact, statistic, or real-life example). Briefly reflect afterward:

- Did this quick step help my idea feel clearer and more convincing?
- Did it boost my confidence in sharing my idea with others?

This habit solidifies your ideas—and your confidence—one step at a time.

Last Call Spark

Your gut can spot something great, but when you support it with proof, others see it too. Pairing instinct with evidence turns good ideas into trusted solutions. That's how you build confidence and a reputation for sound judgment, which will serve you well now and in the future.

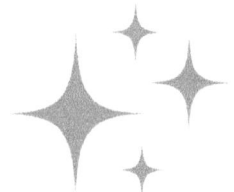

Chapter 6

You Don't Need to Shout to Be Heard: Influence Doesn't Require Volume—Use Your Voice Strategically

Ever seen someone walk into a room and, without raising their voice, immediately command attention? Influence isn't about how loudly you speak—it's about how you speak. Too often, we believe being heard means talking more, when in reality, it's about talking *better*. The most respected professionals don't compete for airtime; they deliver insights that matter. This chapter digs into how you can cultivate presence, choose words that resonate, and ensure your ideas stick—without feeling like you have to shout to be noticed.

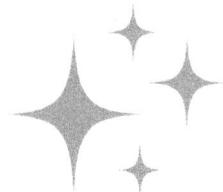

Confessions of a Karaoke Killer

I'll admit it: I've always been a bit of an extroverted introvert. My natural inclination was to stay in the background, playing it safe. But I quickly learned that in a professional setting, being invisible doesn't get you anywhere. So, I trained myself to speak up, step in, and make sure I was heard.

And it worked... until it didn't. My determination to stand out turned into an instinct to take control. I was always ready to make my mark, sometimes at the expense of making space for others. That's when I realized: real influence isn't about being the loudest. It's about knowing when to speak, when to listen, and how to make room for voices beyond your own.

Why Thoughtful Speaking is More Powerful Than Loud Talking

★ **Clarity Cuts Through the Noise**
A well-placed, insightful comment holds more weight than a flood of words. Speak with intention, and people will listen.

★ **Being Measured Earns Respect**
When you speak only when it adds value, your voice carries more authority. Thoughtfulness beats volume every time.

- **Well-Timed Words Get Noticed**

  The quieter, confident voices often leave the biggest impact. When you choose your moments wisely, your words stand out.

- **Influence Comes from Presence, Not Just Speaking**

  Being known as someone who listens and contributes meaningfully earns you more respect than always trying to have the last word.

- **Your Strength is in What You Say, Not How Loudly You Say It**

  True power doesn't come from dominating a conversation – it comes from making others want to hear what you have to say.

My Own Lesson: Adjusting the Volume for Maximum Impact

When I was asked to lead a high-stakes global conference, I was determined to make it a blockbuster success. With 300+ attendees and a strong volunteer team, I had a vision: a flawless event that would impress leadership and set the tone for our department's culture.

I went all in: managing every detail, making every decision, and keeping everything on my track. The problem? I became so laser-focused on execution that I didn't see what was happening around me. My team had great ideas that I barely acknowledged because they didn't fit my plan. Without meaning to, I had steamrolled the very people I was leading.

The event was a huge success. Everything ran smoothly, and the feedback was glowing. But later, I found out that some of my team felt sidelined. They didn't feel heard, and the experience, while rewarding, hadn't been as collaborative.

That stung. I had achieved my goal, but at what cost?

The Lesson Earned

I thought leadership meant owning and executing the vision. But real leadership? It's about making space for others.

I had been so focused on impact that I missed the chance to bring my team along. And truthfully, if I had listened more, maybe the event could have been even better.

Now, I know real influence isn't about taking center stage; it's about lifting others up with you.

Case Study 1: Steering the Room Without Yanking the Wheel

Stage Setting

Dylan had just been promoted to HR lead for a cross-functional staff development initiative. She was excited but quickly felt out of her depth: meetings were filled with dominant personalities, and she found it difficult to insert herself into fast-moving discussions. She worried that if she wasn't vocal enough, her ideas would get lost.

Spark Moment

During a particularly heated meeting, Dylan tried to jump in multiple times but struggled to shift the conversation. Meanwhile, a senior colleague who spoke sparingly managed to steer the discussion with just a few well-placed comments. Dylan realized that influence wasn't just about talking—it was about knowing when and how to contribute.

Path to Thrive

Instead of pushing to speak more, Dylan focused on speaking with purpose. She prepared key insights ahead of time and chose moments to ask questions that steered the discussion rather than added to the noise.

Gradually, she noticed people responding differently: her comments carried more weight, and team members started making room for her input.

Time to Shine

By the end of the project, Dylan still wasn't the loudest in the room, but her influence had grown. Her ability to contribute and connect the dots led to better team conversations. Dylan learned that you get better results by steering the conversation in your favor.

Case Study 2: When Talking Too Much Drowned Out the Win

Stage Setting

Tanya, a driven sales associate, was known for her high energy and big ideas. When her company launched a new product, the sales team held brainstorming sessions to develop creative marketing strategies. Tanya saw this as a chance to stand out, so she jumped into every meeting ready to pitch bold suggestions.

Spark Moment

After one particularly fast-paced discussion, a teammate casually remarked, "It's tough to get a word in around here," clearly pointing to Tanya. She was caught off guard. She thought she was being engaged and enthusiastic. But when she reflected, she realized she had been dominating the conversation without meaning to.

Path to Thrive

Determined to adjust, Tanya tried to listen more and

speak less, but it didn't feel natural. She was mostly holding back, afraid of repeating the same mistake. In one meeting, she stayed so quiet that her manager later asked why she hadn't said a word.

Tanya realized she had swung too far in the opposite direction. The goal wasn't to go silent—it was to strike a balance between contributing and making space for others. Slowly, she started experimenting: instead of rushing to be first, she picked her moments more carefully and asked teammates follow-up questions to encourage discussion.

Time to Shine

The shift wasn't immediate, but over time, Tanya started finding her rhythm. Her big ideas didn't go away, but now she worked on reading the room before jumping in. Some days, she still caught herself talking over others, but she improved at self-correction.

Tanya learned that influence isn't about taking up the most space—it's about knowing when to step forward and when to step back.

Case Study 3: The Volume Check That Finally Got Heard

Stage Setting

Sophie, a junior analyst in the accounting department, had a sharp eye for spotting mistakes and inefficiencies. Any time she saw an issue—big or small—she flagged it. She thought she was being helpful, but over time, colleagues started tuning her out. Instead of being seen as a problem-solver, she had unintentionally earned a reputation as "the office megaphone."

Spark Moment

One day, Sophie pointed out a minor process inefficiency in a meeting, expecting appreciation for her diligence. Instead, her manager looked unimpressed. Later, in private, her manager told her: "I value your attention to detail, but if you flag every little thing, it's hard to know what actually matters." That hit hard. She wasn't trying to nitpick. She was just trying to help.

Path to Thrive

Sophie had to rework her approach. Instead of immediately raising every issue, she started working with her manager to categorize concerns into urgent, important, and minor buckets. She also observed how senior colleagues handled similar situations: they didn't just point out problems but framed them with possible solutions.

Time to Shine

Over time, and with lots of effort, Sophia's reputation shifted. Instead of being known as an alarmist, she was acknowledged for her ability to spot and prioritize critical concerns. She learned that speaking

> up is valuable—but knowing when and how to speak up is what makes influence stick.

Let's reflect on how to use your voice with intention, clarity, and influence—no shouting required.

1. True to You Check-In

Your voice is like an artist's brushstroke—it's not about how many strokes you make, but how thoughtfully you place each one. Choosing words intentionally paints a clear, powerful picture, making your input memorable and respected.

Something to Try:

Reflect briefly on a recent work interaction:

- Was my input meaningful and clear, or did I speak just to fill silence?
- How might simplifying my message make it resonate more strongly?
- What's one small adjustment to help my ideas land clearly next time?

Quick notes help sharpen your communication style.

2. Stay in Sync Tracker

Effective influence means knowing when your voice matters most—and when it's best to pause or step back, especially if tensions or conflict arise. Thoughtful decisions about when and how you engage help maintain your credibility and build trust, even in tricky conversations.

Something to Try:

After conversations (especially ones in which there was tension or disagreement), briefly reflect:

- Did I consciously decide to speak up, stay quiet, or encourage someone else's voice in moments of tension?
- Were there situations when speaking less actually helped defuse potential conflict?
- What's one practical way I can thoughtfully manage my voice next time I sense conflict arising?

Quick reflections build your confidence navigating tougher moments.

3. Shine Prompt

Listening deeply isn't passive—it's a power move. Being fully present when others speak lets you respond with clarity, depth, and genuine impact, making your words stronger and your presence felt.

Something to Try:

Pick one conversation and practice "power listening":

- Fully tune in, absorbing what others say without immediately planning your reply.
- Wait for a clear pause before responding, ensuring your input directly addresses or adds to what was shared.

Afterward, quickly reflect:

- Did my careful listening enhance the conversation quality?
- Did my input carry more weight because it directly connected to others' ideas?

Brief reflections help your voice become more strategic and impactful.

Draft, Don't Detonate

Sometimes you need to scream before you can sing. Hit Reply, then immediately erase all names for the To and CC lines. Vent away. Breathe. Then rewrite with a calm mind and steady hand.

Last Call Spark

Influence isn't loud; it's intentional. When you speak with purpose, listen fully, and pick your moments wisely, people pay attention. You don't have to take up more space to make an impact; you just need to use yours well.

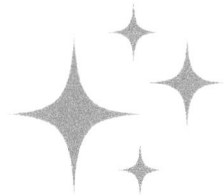

Chapter 7

Recognize Your Limits, Reach New Heights: Grow Beyond Your Current Limits While Avoiding Burnout

It's easy to glorify pushing yourself to the limit, but what happens when the limit pushes back? Growth happens when we stretch ourselves, but burnout happens when we ignore our capacity. Knowing your limits isn't about holding back—it's about understanding when to accelerate and when to recharge. Think of boundaries as the foundation that helps you reach higher, not barriers that hold you back. This chapter explores how to expand your capabilities while ensuring you don't sacrifice your well-being in the process.

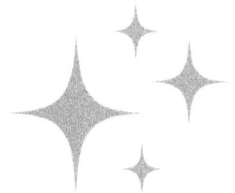

Confessions of a Gold Star Chaser

I loved being the one who pulled off the impossible. Event planning was one of the biggest stars in my wheelhouse, and I chased bigger, better results every time. Success wasn't just a goal. It was my fuel.

But the pursuit of perfection came at a cost. I ignored my own limits, convinced that if I just pushed harder, I could make anything happen. The real lesson? Growth isn't about stretching yourself to the breaking point—it's about knowing when to push and when to pause.

Why Knowing Your Limits Helps You Soar

★ **Boundaries Are the Secret to Sustainable Success**

Limits aren't barriers; they're guides that keep you from stretching too thin. Knowing where to focus your energy helps you go further, not just faster.

★ **Pushing Too Hard Can Backfire**

Growth happens outside your comfort zone, but overextending yourself leads to exhaustion. Smart professionals know when to stretch and when to step back.

- **Quality Beats Quantity Every Time**
  Spreading yourself too thin results in doing a lot of things okay, rather than a few things exceptionally. Prioritize what moves the needle.

- **Knowing When to Say No Builds Confidence**
  Saying no isn't a weakness. It's a smart maneuver. Protect your time and energy whenever possible, helping others (and you) value your contributions.

- **Success is a Marathon, Not a Sprint**
  Pacing yourself ensures you don't burn out before you reach your biggest goals. Smart growth is about sustainability, not just speed.

My Own Lesson: When Firing on All Cylinders Backfired

I had planned divisional sales kickoff events before, but always as part of a team. This time? It was all on me.

It wasn't like I wanted to do everything alone. Therejust wasn't anyone else available. The event had to happen, and I had to make it work. So, I threw myself into the project, determined to hit it out of the park, convinced that if I just worked hard enough, I could pull it off.

The warning signs were there: the schedule was packed too tightly, some speakers were underprepared, and I was running on fumes. But instead of raising the flag, I doubled down, believing that if I just kept pushing, everything would come together.

It didn't.

The event fell flat. The packed agenda left the audience drained, the speakers struggled, and by mid-session, people started leaving early. My boss, always supportive, later gave me honest feedback: "I know you worked hard, but in the end, we didn't deliver. This event was a D-."

I realized I had missed the mark in multiple ways. I couldn't magically create more resources, but I could have flagged the risks earlier, built in buffers, and set more realistic expectations instead of trying to muscle through.

The Lesson Earned

I thought rising to the tall challenge would prove my worth. Well, I learned the hard way that burning out isn't a badge of honor but a blind spot.

There wasn't a magic solution to get more help, but there was a way to set expectations better. I had been so focused on making it all work that I ignored my real options—flagging risks earlier and recognizing when things weren't realistic instead of hoping my sheer willpower would make them work.

That was a big lesson about growth not meaning just to take on challenges but to take them on smartly. Strength isn't measured by how much you push; it's measured by knowing when to step back and recalibrate.

Case Study 1: How Playing It Safe Shrank the Field

Stage Setting

Mia had always been praised for being thoughtful and reliable. As a new business analyst at a midsize tech firm, she took pride in doing her work thoroughly and meeting every expectation. She preferred to keep her head down and her to-do list tight, believing that quality spoke louder than visibility.

When cross-functional projects popped up, she politely declined or stayed quiet, convincing herself she wasn't ready yet and didn't want to risk failure in a public forum.

Spark Moment

During a quarterly team sync, Mia's manager asked why she hadn't joined any of the broader initiatives happening across teams. Mia gave a vague answer about staying focused. But the question stuck with her, and so did the subtle shift in her manager's tone.

Later, a more junior colleague volunteered for a stretch assignment—and did a great job and got much kudos. Mia realized she'd been so focused on staying in her comfort zone that she hadn't given herself the chance to grow.

Path to Thrive

Mia knew she had to shift. At the next opportunity, she raised her hand to support a cross-team pilot project—not lead it but contribute. The learning curve was steep, and her voice didn't always carry in meetings, but she asked questions, offered insights when she had them, and slowly built confidence.

She made a few missteps along the way, including misinterpreting a data requirement that caused confusion, but she owned it and adjusted quickly. The world didn't end, and her team appreciated her willingness to jump in and learn.

Time to Shine

Mia didn't crush the project. She still hesitated in meetings and sometimes stayed quiet when she had something useful to say. But she showed up, made small contributions, and asked for feedback.

When the project wrapped, her manager told her she was glad to see Mia stepping into new territory. "You've got more to offer than you think," she said.

Mia wasn't sure she felt that quite yet, but she happily accepted the compliment.

Case Study 2: The Implosion of Perfectionism

Stage Setting

Bridget, a junior data analyst at a financial firm, prided herself on being precise and dependable. But behind her polished exterior, Bridget was quietly unraveling.

What no one saw were the 11 p.m. Slack messages, skipped lunches, and endless weekends reviewing spreadsheet macros just to make sure everything was "perfect." She didn't want to say no or admit she was struggling. She thought pushing through was the professional thing to do.

Spark Moment

When her manager assigned her a fast-turnaround dashboard for a leadership meeting, Bridget went all in... and completely wiped out. She submitted the file on time but forgot to refresh a data pull, meaning two key charts were incorrect. The execs caught it mid-meeting. She could feel the blood draining from her head. She'd made her first public mistake.

Path to Thrive

Shaken, Bridget called a mentor she trusted. The mentor didn't focus on the error but on the pressure Bridget was putting on herself. "You're treating every task like a final exam," she said. "Part of doing your job is knowing when to take a breath and ask for help."

Bridget opened up to her manager, and together, they created checkpoints on major projects and designated "review buddies" to catch small errors before submission. Most importantly, Bridget began practicing something new: giving herself a limit on how long to "polish."

Time to Shine

Bridget didn't win any awards for her next project. But she stopped triple-checking every detail at 2 a.m., and when a teammate asked if she needed help, she actually said yes.

Bridget realized she didn't need to be perfect—just present, prepared, and willing to keep learning. She still caught herself spiraling sometimes, but now she knew how to pause and course-correct. It wasn't polished growth. It was progress.

Case Study 3: When Big Ambitions Outran the Plan

Stage Setting

Emma, fresh out of college, landed her first job as an operations associate. She thrived on pressure and wanted to prove she was ready for more. So when her manager floated the idea of her leading a high-priority initiative coordinating multiple teams, she said yes without hesitation, despite having zero experience managing cross-functional projects.

Spark Moment

The excitement faded fast. Emma was spending hours chasing status updates, forgetting follow-ups, and missing small details that had big consequences. When a senior team member flagged a mistake in front of the group, her confidence wobbled. She worried she was in over her head but didn't want to give up. She wasn't sure what was worse: quitting halfway or failing quietly.

Path to Thrive

Eventually, she booked a check-in with her supervisor and admitted she was overwhelmed. To her surprise, he was understanding and encouraging. He helped create a more structured plan and paired her with a peer who had led a similar initiative the year before. Emma internally resented this at first, still hoping she could "power through" alone, but gradually she leaned into the support system.

Time to Shine

The project wrapped up slightly behind schedule, with mixed feedback. Emma felt disappointed as it hadn't gone the way she'd hoped.

But she didn't avoid the debrief. She showed up, owned her missteps, and listened. She hadn't nailed it right off the bat, but she was still in the game, a little wiser and a lot more grounded.

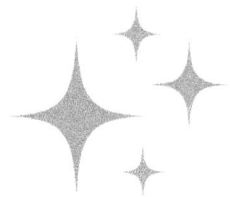

Here are a few ways to reflect on your current capacity and stretch in a way that's healthy, not overwhelming.

1. True to You Check-In

Career growth shouldn't feel like endlessly stacking plates—it should feel more like planting seeds you genuinely want to see bloom. Regularly checking which skills excite you (and which don't) helps you nurture the right seeds, making your growth purposeful, manageable, and fun.

Something to Try:

Reflect briefly on recent tasks or projects:

- Which skill felt genuinely fun or exciting to use recently and deserves more nurturing?
- Is there a skill I'm "watering" regularly but doesn't feel rewarding?
- What's a quick, realistic action I can take soon (like reading something interesting or talking with someone skilled) to nurture the growth I genuinely care about?

Brief journal notes keep your garden growing happily.

2. Stay in Sync Tracker

Early in your career, your workload can sometimes feel like luggage someone else packed—heavier than you'd prefer, and not always in your control. It's normal to have moments when you're simply paying your dues or building your foundation. Even when you can't choose every task, becoming aware of your limits and proactively clarifying expectations helps you grow stronger, manage your energy, and develop skills you'll rely on throughout your career.

Something to Try:

Briefly reflect on your current responsibilities:

- Does my workload currently feel manageable, or am I in a period of heavier pressure that's part of building my foundation?
- Even if I can't lighten my load directly, could I clarify expectations or priorities to handle it more comfortably?
- What's one practical insight or strength I've gained from managing a challenging workload, like better prioritization, clearer communication, or learning to ask for support when needed?

Quick reflections help you build resilience and manage your workload, even when the pressures of the job are beyond your control.

3. Shine Prompt

Real growth isn't just about skills or managing tasks—it's also about building confidence through small, daily victories. Tiny acts of courage each day slowly stretch your limits without feeling stressful, helping you become comfortable stepping into new experiences over time.

Something to Try:

Today, pick one small, comfortable-but-courageous action—like asking a quick question you've hesitated about, speaking briefly in a meeting, or volunteering to help in a simple, new way. Afterward, briefly reflect:

- Did this small act feel empowering, encouraging, or enlightening?
- Did it boost my confidence or make taking future steps feel easier?

Small daily stretches turn courage into your everyday habit.

Last Call Spark

Doing too much can leave you running on empty. Doing too little can keep you parked at the gate. Real growth doesn't come from maxing out or holding back . It comes from finding your pace, knowing when to throttle forward, and learning when to pull over and reset. That's how you build strength that lasts and a journey worth staying on.

Chapter 8

Leverage Your Unique Toolkit: Identify and Maximize Your Distinct Strengths for Lasting Success

Imagine walking into a new challenge with a bag packed just for you, filled with tools perfectly suited for what's ahead. That's what happens when you understand and use your strengths strategically. You don't need to master everything; you just need to leverage what makes you unique. This chapter helps you identify, sharpen, and confidently apply your skills so you can stand out in a way that feels natural, effective, and sustainable.

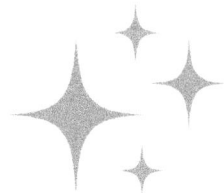

Confessions of a Wordsmith in a Numbers World

Spreadsheets and I were not meant to be. As a music major turned business professional, I assumed I'd always stick to words, not numbers.

Then came the job that forced me to dive headfirst into sales metrics, pivot tables, and formulas. At first, I resisted. Then, I adapted. And to my surprise, I got good at it. I learned that strengths aren't just what you start with. They'rehey're what you build along the way.

Why Owning Your Strengths Sets You Apart

- **You Don't Have to Be Good at Every Single Thing**

  Instead of fixing every weakness, double down on what makes you shine. Mastering your strengths creates more impact than being average at everything.

- **Your Unique Skills Give You a Competitive Edge**

  No one else has your exact mix of experiences, talents, and perspectives. That's not a flaw—it's your greatest asset.

- **Confidence Comes from Competence**
  The better you know your strengths, the more naturally confidence follows. Owning your expertise makes you a go-to person in your field.

- **Skills Can Be Learned, but Strengths Are Your Superpower**
  You can always pick up new knowledge, but your natural abilities set you apart. Lean into what feels exciting and motivates you.

- **Your Toolkit Evolves—Keep Adding to It**
  Staying ahead means constantly refining and expanding your strengths. Growth isn't about becoming someone else but about maximizing who you already are.

My Own Lesson: From Spreadsheet Stumbles to a Standout Win

I had just stepped into a sales operations role when I was handed a high-pressure project: creating a ranking system for hundreds of salespeople. This was going to be displayed in front of the entire team. And if it had errors? Never mind my own humiliation—it would affect the credibility of our whole management system.

The problem? I wasn't a numbers person. Building macros in Excel? This was way outside my comfort zone. My first attempts were full of errors, and I could feel panic creeping in.

I was baked into a corner, and I had to play to my strengths: communication and relationship-building. I reached out to the spreadsheet wizards on my team, leaned on my logic skills, and learned just enough to get the job done accurately.

Launch day arrived. The rankings displayed perfectly. No errors. No disasters. Just relief and pride.

The Lesson Earned

I thought not being a numbers person meant I wasn't cut out for this project. But success comes from knowing how to figure things out, not from knowing everything in the first place.

By leaning into my strengths—communication, problem-solving, and asking the right people for help—I built something I never thought I could.

Turns out, you don't have to be an expert in everything. You just have to know how to use what you've got to learn what you don't.

Case Study 1: How a Fresh Perspective Created Clarity

Stage Setting

Stephanie had just joined the marketing strategy team at a growing health tech company. She was used to fast-paced content work and had a sharp eye for design and detail. But when she was asked to lead a competitive insights presentation for the executive team, she felt out of her depth. The research involved loads of complex data, industry jargon, and unfamiliar frameworks, nothing like her usual creative work.

Spark Moment

As she sifted through spreadsheets and market briefs, she felt overwhelmed. Every document felt disjointed, and she struggled to find a coherent thread. Then it hit her: if she was this lost, the execs probably would be too. Instead of forcing herself to become a data expert overnight, Stephanie leaned into what she did know: how to make information visual, digestible, and meaningful.

Path to Thrive

Stephanie spent time distilling the insights down to core patterns and key messages, and then built a visual story: competitor maps, simplified data graphics, and a clear narrative arc. She pulled in a colleague from product for fact-checking but took ownership of how the message would land.

At first, she worried her approach might seem too "basic." But when she previewed the slides with her manager, the feedback was immediate: "This actually makes sense now."

Time to Shine

Stephanie's presentation wasn't flashy, and she still stumbled through a couple of tough follow-up questions. But her visuals helped the team stay focused, and several execs nodded along. Afterward, her manager sent a quick Slack message: "Nice job! Really clean and easy to follow."

It wasn't a standing ovation, but it was the first time Stephanie saw how her way of thinking added real value—not because she knew everything, but because she helped others make sense of it.

Case Study 2: When Style Needed Substance

Stage Setting

Kyla, a high-energy salesperson, had just moved into a customer success role. Her charisma and quick thinking had always been her standout differentiators. But in a job that was all about listening, empathy, and long-term trust, those strengths started to fall flat.

Spark Moment

Kyla launched into her usual rhythm: fast-paced

calls, enthusiastic pitches, high-energy check-ins. But instead of strengthening accounts, she was getting cold responses. One client said, “I don’t need a sales pitch. I need a partner.” That stung. A lot.

Path to Thrive

Kyla started recording her calls and listening back. What she heard was eye-opening: she was filling silence instead of making space. She began making adjustments: slowing down, preparing better questions, and using her natural energy to stay engaged rather than dominate.

Time to Shine

Her interactions weren’t all perfect, but they became more productive. Clients started looping her in earlier, and one even called her “a lifesaver” when she proactively helped resolve a key issue. Kyla didn’t throw out her personality; she learned how to use it with intention.

Case Study 3: The Shift That Brought Order to Chaos

Stage Setting

Denise was used to moving fast. As a product manager, she thrived on action, ideas, and momentum. But a major product launch with multiple teams left her drowning in chaos—updates flying in, missed details, and stress running high.

Spark Moment

Emails were piling up. Slack pings never stopped. Denise was jumping from fire to fire, barely pausing for bathroom breaks. Then one night, she sent out a production update with the wrong deadline, causing a scramble on the manufacturing side and a tense call with the ops lead.

She didn't sleep much that night. She had a nagging feeling that she was actually the one creating the chaos.

Path to Thrive

The next morning, Denise wrote down everything she was juggling and realized she wasn't just busy, she was reactive. She couldn't control everything, but she could do better with how she managed her day.

She started setting aside 10 minutes each morning to prioritize her tasks before opening her inbox. She added a tracker to keep tabs on open items and set calendar reminders to review key deliverables before deadlines. It wasn't fancy, but it helped her breathe.

She also mentioned the recent mix-up to her manager, who suggested adding a standing weekly check-in with the team, something Denise hadn't felt empowered to propose herself.

Time to Shine

Denise didn't magically become the most organized person on the team, but things started to feel less chaotic. She caught issues earlier, felt more in control, and wasn't constantly bracing for something to fall through the cracks.

During her next 1:1, her manager said, "I can tell you're getting a handle on things. Good job." Denise learned that a simple system could be just as powerful as any skill, especially when it helped her stay grounded.

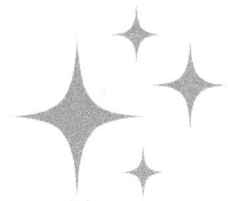

It's time to take inventory of the strengths that make you you—and how to grow them even further.

1. True to You Check-In

Your unique toolkit isn't just about refining what you're already good at. It's also about recognizing areas outside your comfort zone where your natural strengths can help you grow. Checking in regularly helps you confidently stretch into new skills, even those that feel unfamiliar or challenging.

Something to Try:

Briefly reflect on recent experiences:

- Which familiar skills felt uniquely satisfying and aligned to me?
- Did I recently face a task or project requiring a skill that felt uncomfortable or outside my usual strengths?
- How could my existing strengths support me in growing this uncomfortable skill further?

Quick notes help you turn uncomfortable challenges into empowering growth opportunities.

2. Stay in Sync Tracker

Your uniqueness is amplified when you tap into others who complement your talents. Recognizing who uniquely complements your strengths helps you build a network that maximizes both your impact and theirs.

Something to Try:

Briefly consider colleagues or connections around you:

- Who uniquely enhances or complements my skillset, making our combined strengths even stronger?
- Have I recently leveraged these complementary relationships intentionally?
- What's one quick action to strengthen these unique partnerships—like checking in, sharing insights, or collaborating briefly?

Simple reflections ensure your unique toolkit is strengthened by equally unique partnerships.

3. Shine Prompt

Your strengths don't grow by sitting on a shelf—they grow when you use them, stretch them, and sharpen them. A little bit each day builds fluency, confidence, and momentum. And you don't need hours. Just five focused minutes can reinforce a skill and remind you what's in your toolkit.

Something to Try:

Pick one skill, big or small, that you want to grow this week. Then take one tiny, focused action that exercises it.

Some examples are:

- Working on writing? Try rewording a clunky email into something sharper.
- Strengthening data skills? Spend five minutes learning a new spreadsheet shortcut and using it.
- Want to be a better listener? In your next conversation, try asking one follow-up question before offering your take.

At the end of each exercise, make a quick note:

- What did I stretch or try differently today?
- Did it feel energizing, awkward, or empowering?
- What would I try next?

Your strengths don't have to be polished. They just have to be in play.

When *In Doubt, Go Clear*

Want to sound sharper? Trim the fluff.
Lead with the point. Clarity isn't being curt.
It's what gets your idea across.

Last Call Spark

Your toolkit is made up of skills that best serve you when things get messy, uncertain, or high-stakes. No one else has your exact mix, and no one else sees the road the way you do. When you learn to trust your toolkit, and keep adding to it as you go, you're doing more than staying on track. You're charting a path that's distinctly, confidently yours.

Thrive and SHINE

I

Invest in Growth

Growth doesn't come from playing it safe. It comes from leaning into the unknown, betting on yourself, and learning from every experience: wins, missteps, and everything in between.

Think of your career like a garden. You plant seeds, you nurture them, and over time, you grow. But here's the thing: No two gardens look alike, and no one can tell you exactly how yours should take shape. The best growth happens when you stop following someone else's blueprint and start trusting yourself to build something that feels right for you.

This section is about making growth an intentional investment. We'll dive into curiosity as your greatest fuel, why risks (even the scary ones) are worth taking, and how every relationship—good, bad, or unexpected—teaches you something valuable.

Because real growth is not about ticking off milestones. It's about expanding who you are, what you're capable of, and what you dare to reach for.

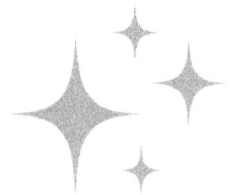

Let's dig in.

Chapter 9

Curiosity is Your Fuel: A Curious Mind Opens Doors to Endless Opportunities

Some people think success comes from always having the answers. But the real game-changer? *Asking the right questions*.

Curiosity isn't just about learning—it's about uncovering possibilities others overlook. Think about it: the people who get ahead aren't just those who know the most; they're the ones willing to explore, experiment, and challenge assumptions.

This chapter is all about tapping into your curiosity, using it as a career accelerator, and making it your secret weapon for continuous growth.

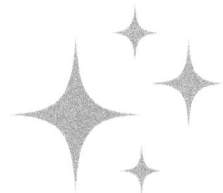

Confessions of a Quietly Curious Mind

I was always curious, always questioning—but rarely out loud. I preferred to observe, reflect, and refine my thoughts before speaking up.

The problem? By the time I was ready to contribute, the moment had passed. I had to learn that curiosity isn't just about having questions—it's about asking them, even when you don't have the perfect words lined up. That's where the real breakthroughs happen.

Why Curiosity Turns the Ordinary into Opportunity

- **Curiosity Unlocks Hidden Possibilities**
  The best ideas start with a simple "What if?" A curious mindset helps you spot solutions, uncover opportunities, and challenge the status quo.

- **Questions Lead to Smarter Moves**
  Instead of taking things at face value, questioning why things work the way they do helps you make more informed, strategic choices.

- **Genuine Interest Builds Stronger Connections**
  People appreciate when you take an authentic interest in their ideas. Asking thoughtful

questions fosters trust and opens unexpected doors.

- **Mistakes Become Launchpads, Not Roadblocks**

  Curiosity turns setbacks into experiments. Instead of seeing failure as a stop sign, see it as a detour to a better solution.

- **Curiosity Keeps You Energized and Evolving**

  Approaching work with a "what can I learn from this?" mindset makes every challenge feel like a new adventure instead of a burden.

My Own Lesson: The Cat Was onto Something

When I worked as an executive assistant to our regional head of sales, I loved the fast-paced environment, but one thing bugged me: the lack of training.

We learned the basics (org charts, phones, systems, tools) but nothing about our products, market strategy, or competitors. Yet, we were supporting sales teams driving major deals. Why weren't we given that same foundational knowledge?

Most admin colleagues shrugged it off. That'shat's how it's been, and no one's getting hurt. But I couldn't let it go. So, I pushed to join the sales training program myself, and boy, was it a game-changer. I learned a ton and realized that if admins had this knowledge from day one, we'd be way more effective.

Armed with my firsthand experience, I pitched a training program for admins and whiteboarded it for my boss, who called my idea "cute." Yup, he actually did, but hey, it wasn't a no. I kept refining, gathering support, and turning it into something real. And when the training was finally rolled out company-wide? It wasn't cute anymore. It moved the needle.

The Lesson Earned

Curiosity isn't just about asking why; it's about taking action when something doesn't add up.

Most people accept the status quo, but sometimes, the simplest question—"Why don't we do this?"—can lead to tangible change. I learned that speaking up, even when no one else does, can create something bigger than imagined.

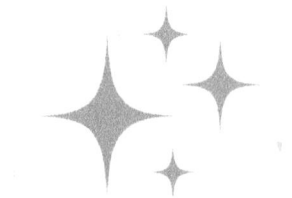

Case Study 1: When a Data Deep Dive Unearthed a Goldmine

Stage Setting

Liz, a marketing associate, was analyzing performance data for the company's latest ad campaign when she spotted something unexpected: manufacturing companies, a sector they hadn't targeted, were engaging at higher rates than their usual tech clients.

Spark Moment

Curious about the anomaly, Liz raised the question in a team meeting: "Could we explore why manufacturing companies are responding so well? Maybe we're missing something." Her manager encouraged her to dig deeper, so she reached out to the sales team for additional insights.

Path to Thrive

Liz discovered that manufacturing clients resonated with certain messaging elements that weren't originally designed for them. She proposed a small test campaign tailored specifically to this industry. While some teammates were skeptical, her data-backed insights helped convince management to give it a shot.

Time to Shine

The campaign performed well, increasing engagement rates by 25% compared to tech-focused campaigns. While it didn't completely shift the company's strategy, it sparked discussions about exploring untapped markets. Liz's curiosity led to real business impact, positioning her as a sharp and resourceful problem-solver.

Case Study 2: The Red Flags Were There but Weren't Seen

Stage Setting
Irene, a frontline community manager, was growing concerned about rising turnover rates in her department. Employees were leaving faster than they could be replaced, and morale among those who stayed seemed to be sinking.

Spark Moment
She had a hunch there was more to the story than exit interviews suggested, but with her growing workload, she hesitated. What if she uncovered something too big to fix? What if leadership already knew? She convinced herself it wasn't urgent—until it was.

Path to Thrive
Months later, several top performers resigned, and productivity plummeted. When leadership finally stepped in, they discovered that poorly communicated workload expectations and pay concerns had been brewing for months. Employees felt unheard, and the damage to morale was significant.

Irene realized that by waiting too long to ask questions, she had missed a chance to get ahead of the issue.

Time to Shine

Determined not to repeat the mistake, Irene introduced pulse surveys and anonymous feedback tools to catch red flags sooner. Over time, these changes rebuilt trust and improved transparency.

She learned that curiosity is more than just asking questions. It's about asking them and taking action before it's too late.

Case Study 3: How One "Why" Turned a Bottleneck into a Breakthrough

Stage Setting

Joanie, a project coordinator at a tech startup, noticed a recurring issue with a current program: deadlines were being missed despite the team working long hours. Something wasn't adding up.

Spark Moment

Instead of assuming the issue was just overwork, Joanie dug into past projects and spotted a pattern: handoffs between departments were unclear, causing tasks to slip through the cracks.

She brought her findings to her manager, suggesting a workflow fix to prevent bottlenecks. Her manager was supportive but warned her that getting buy-in across teams would be a challenge.

Path to Thrive

Encouraged to take the lead, Joanie met with department heads to pitch her workflow improvement. Some teams were receptive; others resisted, arguing that the current system worked "well enough." Instead of pushing, Joanie proposed a small pilot test.

The results showed fewer delays and smoother communication, but convincing the broader organization to change was still an uphill battle.

Time to Shine

Her workflow design wasn't adopted company-wide, but Joanie's initiative didn't go unnoticed. She was later tapped to join a cross-functional process improvement project, positioning her as someone who can bring creative solutions to problems.

She learned that curiosity is just the starting point, and that it needs to be backed up with patience and collaboration, since change doesn't happen overnight.

Let's tap into your natural curiosity and shape it into fuel for real, focused growth.

1. True to You Check-In

Curiosity often lights up like a sparkler—bright, fascinating, but quick to fade if you don't catch it. Using your Work Journal to quickly record these sparks of curiosity ensures they remain visible, ready to inspire future exploration.

Something to Try:

In your Work Journal, set aside a small section to capture your quick "What if...?" or "Why does...?" moments. Every now and then, revisit these sparks and choose one to briefly explore through quick research, a casual chat, or thoughtful reflection.

Quick notes turn passing sparks into lasting insights.

2. Stay in Sync Tracker

Being curious doesn't mean asking every question that pops into your head. Thoughtful curiosity helps you stand out professionally by showing others your questions have purpose, clarity, and genuine value.

Something to Try:

Before asking questions or presenting ideas, pause to reflect:

- Does this question align with my team's objectives, or is it unrelated?
- Would quick research help me ask this question more clearly or effectively?
- Is my curiosity adding clarity or complicating the conversation?

Brief reflections ensure your questions are valued and respected.

3. Shine Prompt

Sometimes the best sparks come when you peek through someone else's window. Observing how others approach their work can illuminate fresh ideas or inspire new ways of thinking about your own challenges.

Something to Try:

Take a quick opportunity to look beyond your usual tasks—chat briefly with someone from another team, watch a different role in action, or join a conversation slightly outside your routine. Afterward, quickly reflect:

- Did this glimpse into another way of working spark a practical idea I can use immediately?
- Did it shift my perspective or inspire a fresh approach to my current tasks?

Small glimpses lead to brighter insights.

Last Call Spark

Curiosity isn't just how you learn—it's how you leave a mark. Asking questions, noticing gaps, and exploring new angles shows initiative, not inexperience. When you stay curious, it's more than just you growing—you help everything around you grow, too.

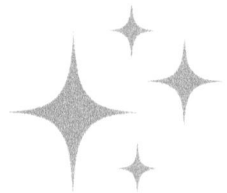

Chapter 10
Bet on Yourself: Take Risks, Trust Your Instincts, and Be Your Own Biggest Advocate

Standing at the edge of a decision, your heart pounds. The safe choice? Step back. The bold choice? Take the leap.

Betting on yourself can feel like reckless risk-taking, but you can cultivate your instincts to know when the leap is worth it. Fear will always be in the background, whispering doubts. But what if, instead of listening to fear, you listened to possibility? This chapter is focused on learning to back yourself—again and again—so you never let hesitation hold you back from opportunities meant for you.

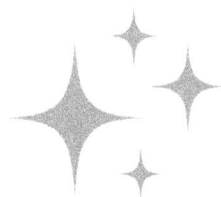

Confessions of a Supernova Control Freak

I looked confident on the outside: fearless, ambitious, always ready to go for it. But inside? I was a mess of worst-case scenarios, overpreparation, and a desperate need to control every outcome.

Spoiler: That's not sustainable. I had to learn the hard way that real confidence doesn't come from having all the answers. It comes from trusting yourself, even when you don't.

Why Bold Moves Build Your Future

★ **Stop Waiting for Permission—Take the Leap**

The biggest opportunities don't come with an official invite. Trust your instincts and take initiative—your future self will thank you.

★ **Stretching Beyond Comfort Expands Your Possibilities**

The more you push your limits, the more you realize you're capable of. Confidence isn't a requirement—it's a result of taking action.

★ **Failure is Just Proof That You're Trying**

No one wins without a few losses. Every

stumble is an investment in your long-term growth.

★ **You Control Your Career Story**

The risks you take today define the stories you tell tomorrow. The most successful careers aren't handed out—they're built with intention.

★ **Confidence is Contagious—Lead by Example**

When you advocate for yourself, others take notice. Your belief in your own potential sets the stage for others to believe in you too.

My Own Lesson: From Shut Down to Leveling Up

I was in a senior analyst role when my manager left, opening the door for a promotion. I was ready. Or at least, I thought I was.

The catch? My VP was very by-the-book, and he was set on an external hire. I went for it anyway, prepped hard, built my case, rehearsed my pitch.

The verdict? He "admired the hell out of my ambition" but didn't think I was ready.

Outwardly, I smiled. Inwardly? Fuming. I knew I could kill it in this role. But I begrudgingly had to admit he wasn't entirely off-base. I hadn't worked closely enough with him to prove my capabilities.

I swallowed my pride and thanked him for the opportunity to interview. I then focused on getting even better while keeping my eyes open for the next shot.

Six months later, a bigger role at HQ opened. I almost didn't apply as fear of rejection lingered, but I went for it. And this time? Got the job, leapfrogging two levels.

The Lesson Earned

Rejection isn't a dead end; it's just redirection.

I could have let that "no" shake my confidence. Instead, I let it fuel my next move. I sharpened my skills, stayed ready, and when the right opportunity came, I was overprepared and unstoppable.

A rejection doesn't mean you're not good enough. It means you're not done yet.

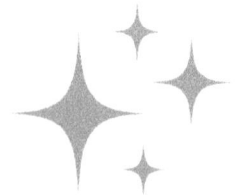

Case Study 1: When a Technical Expert Took the Business Reins

Stage Setting

Vanessa, a data scientist at a healthcare startup, was known for translating complex data into actionable insights. When the company announced a first-line manager role to oversee a new AI-powered product, she was intrigued.

Spark Moment

Despite her technical expertise, Vanessa hesitated. She'd never officially led a team before, and the role required coordinating engineers, designers, and stakeholders. But when she reflected on past projects, she realized she had already been informally guiding teams but hadn't seen herself as a leader yet.

Path to Thrive

Vanessa prepared extensively to make sure she had a strong case. She drafted a detailed proposal outlining her technical vision and how she would collaborate cross-functionally. To bridge her knowledge gaps, she sought advice from colleagues in leadership roles and practiced framing her expertise in a leadership context.

Time to Shine

Her preparation paid off. After multiple interview rounds, Vanessa got the job. The transition wasn't seamless—balancing management with technical work was an adjustment—but her ability to blend technical expertise with empathy and communication made her a standout hire. The product launched successfully, and Vanessa was recognized as a rising star in the department.

Case Study 2: When Fear Spoke Louder Than Opportunity

Stage Setting

Cassie, a talented graphic designer, was known for producing stunning creative work. When her manager announced an opportunity to become part of the account team for an extremely high-profile client, her colleagues encouraged her to go for it. But Cassie wasn't sure she was ready.

Spark Moment

She spent hours debating whether to go for it. What if I fail? What if they compare me to more outgoing designers? What if the client is too tough to work with? Instead of taking the leap, she convinced herself to wait for another shot she felt more "ready" for.

Path to Thrive

Weeks later, the designer spot on the account team went to an external candidate, someone who didn't know the brand or the client as well as Cassie did. Even though she logically knew a move like this was a real possibility, seeing it actually happen still felt like a blow.

Time to Shine
Watching someone else take the spot, Cassie realized she hadn't lost because she wasn't ready; she lost because she never tried. She had let fear and comparison hold her back instead of advocating for herself.

Frustrated but determined, she made a commitment to not sit on the sidelines when an opportunity arose. She started raising her hand to interface more regularly with external clients and partners, speaking up in meetings, and pushing herself into situations that stretched her confidence.

Case Study 3: When a Setback Became the Ultimate Setup

Stage Setting
Zoe, an HR generalist, was great at connecting with employees and solving workplace challenges. When a senior HR manager position opened, she applied with confidence, assuming her strong reputation would carry her through.

Spark Moment
During the interview, she quickly realized she wasn't ready for the strategic side of the role. Questions about workforce planning and executive negotiations

left her scrambling for answers. She excelled at employee relations, but the hiring panel didn't see the broader vision they needed.

Path to Thrive

Zoe didn't get the job, and the feedback was tough: she wasn't strategic enough for the next level. Instead of dwelling on disappointment, she made a plan. She enrolled in an HR certification program, shadowed her manager on executive projects, and contributed to high-level discussions.

Time to Shine

When the next senior HR position opened internally, someone else got the job. Instead of waiting for another internal job to open up, Zoe applied elsewhere.

Her expanded skill set impressed hiring teams at a competitor, and she landed the senior HR manager role she had worked so hard for. Missing the first opportunity wasn't a dead end. It was the push she needed to grow into the right role.

You've got what it takes. These checkpoints will help you build the courage to keep choosing yourself—on purpose.

1. True to You Check-In

Backing yourself is about trusting that you bring something valuable to the table. But let's be real: sometimes self-doubt sneaks in. Regular check-ins are like recharging your own battery, reminding you of your strengths, your progress, and your potential.

Something to Try:

Look back on a moment when you spoke up, took a risk, or put yourself out there:

- What made me step up in that moment?
- Did it remind me of a strength I tend to overlook?
- How can I carry this insight forward to advocate for myself more next time?

Think of it as saving those moments in your personal highlight reel. You'll want to rewatch them when the next challenge comes.

2. Stay in Sync Tracker

In the early stages of your career, it's easy to feel like you're racing ahead without checking the rearview mirror. But when you pause to track your small leaps—whether graceful or a bit wobbly—you start to see just how far you've come.

Something to Try:

In your Work Journal, start a "Took the Leap" log:

- What action or risk did I take?
- What did I expect to happen, and what actually happened?
- Did this move me closer to a goal, teach me something new, or show I'm more capable than I thought?

Looking back at your leaps helps you stay grounded while you grow.

3. Shine Prompt

Confidence doesn't come from waiting until you feel ready—it comes from motion. Small, daily steps into discomfort build the courage to take bigger leaps when it counts.

Something to Try:

Choose one simple way today to put yourself in motion—share an idea, ask a question, try something new. Later, reflect:

- How did it feel to stretch yourself a little today?
- Did it make the next step feel less intimidating?

Tiny moves forward build momentum, and that's what turns hesitation into confidence.

Flip the Switch Yourself

Nobody knows you like you do.
Don't settle in like a passenger.
You're the one who brings the spark.
Turn on the light, and step into what's next.

Last Call Spark

Taking risks doesn't mean always knowing where you'll land. It means trusting you'll figure it out when you get there. Every time you speak up, step forward, or choose yourself, you're not just taking a risk—you're rewriting what you believe you're capable of.

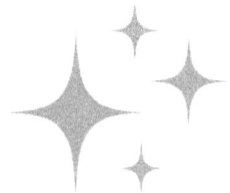

Chapter 11

No Relationship Is Wasted: Every Connection Contributes to Your Growth in Unexpected Ways

Think back to the people who've crossed your professional path—the ones who lifted you up, the ones who challenged you, and even the ones who made things difficult. Every single relationship holds value, whether it's a direct opportunity or a lesson learned. The key is recognizing these connections for what they offer, even if they don't fit the traditional mentor or advocate mold. This chapter explores how to make the most of your professional relationships, expected or not, and why investing in people always pays off.

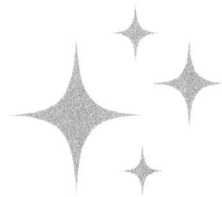

Confessions of a Judgey Queen

I prided myself on being observant, watching how people presented themselves, handled pressure, and framed their ideas. And honestly? I made snap judgments faster than a reality show judge. In my head, I sorted people: brilliant, unreliable, overconfident, too passive.

Looking back, I cringe. The people I overlooked? Many turned out to be the most valuable allies. The ones I dismissed? Some of them taught me lessons I didn't even know I needed. Turns out, respect isn't earned by being right about people—it's earned by giving them a real chance before making up your mind.

My Own Lesson: Opposites Assigned, Respect Aligned

In my business development role, I was paired with the head of product management, who was brilliant but brutally direct. She marched to her own drumbeat.

If I was fast-paced and gut-driven, she was methodical and analytical. Conversations were blunt, no small talk. I'd ask for quick factoids, and she'd respond with questions instead. We sometimes talked over each other.

Frustration built up on both sides. But avoiding her wasn't an option as she was my only source for product messaging. So, I shifted gears. Instead of pushing for fast answers, I adjusted—asked broader questions, left space for her process, reworked timelines. It wasn't perfect, but we made it work.

We never became close. When the project ended, I assumed that was it.

Years later, when I was unexpectedly laid off, she was one of the first to reach out. She offered connections and encouragement, which is something I never saw coming.

The Lesson Earned

Some relationships will be hard, but that doesn't mean they won't matter.

I used to think tough work relationships were just obstacles to get through, but even the difficult ones can leave an imprint. The people who frustrate you? They can sharpen your skills. The ones who seem indifferent? They might be paying closer attention than you think.

I never expected this colleague to show up for me when I needed it most. But that's the thing about relationships: you don't always see their value until the moment it matters.

Case Study 1: When Standing Out Made Room to be Seen

Stage Setting

Quinn, a junior graphic designer, didn't exactly blend in at her sleek creative agency. Her style was unapologetically bold—bright colors, glittery accessories, and a vintage vibe that seemed lifted straight from another era. She brought that same flair to her desk, her designs, and her presence.

While no one said anything outright, Quinn often felt the looks—the second glances in meetings, the extra explanations clients asked for when she was in the room. She knew her style sometimes made people underestimate her. But she also knew she was good at what she did.

Spark Moment

When Quinn was pulled into a high-stakes campaign, she was paired with a senior colleague known for being polished, strategic, and clearly skeptical of her. During their early meetings, Maya could feel the hesitation; feedback came in cautious tones.

But as the work progressed, Quinn's unconventional ideas began to unlock fresh creative directions the team hadn't considered. Slowly, the dynamic shifted.

Path to Thrive

Their collaboration was brief, but Quinn made an impression. The senior colleague noted her contributions in a performance review, highlighting her originality and creative instincts. While they didn't become close collaborators, the experience gave Quinn a glimpse of how perceptions could change when she let her work speak.

Time to Shine

Months later, Quinn was asked to join a new pitch team by someone she didn't even realize had been watching her work. Her name had come up as someone who "thinks outside the box," and that was exactly what the team needed.

It wasn't a direct line from one project to the next. But it was proof that showing up fully, even when you feel out of place, can plant seeds you don't see until they bloom.

Case Study 2: The Redlines that Rewrote Her Thinking

Stage Setting

Adrienne had just landed her first full-time role as an events coordinator at a small but high-profile agency. Her new manager was known for being sharp, fast-paced, and demanding. She wasn't unkind, but she had little time for handholding and expected new hires to keep up.

In early meetings, Adrienne noticed her suggestions were often met with rapid-fire questions or redirected entirely. No one ever said she was doing poorly, but she knew she wasn't acing her job.

Spark Moment

One day, Adrienne submitted a draft event plan that she'd worked hard on, only to get it back heavily marked up with a short note: "Need tighter flow. Better risk mitigation. We've covered this before."

Adrienne had done what she thought was right, but clearly, it hadn't landed. She realized that what had worked in college (being enthusiastic and a fast learner) wasn't enough here. She needed to anticipate the standard, understand what mattered, and learn to deliver work that could stand on its own.

Path to Thrive

Adrienne started watching how her manager worked: what she prioritized, how she structured presentations, what kinds of questions she asked. She began running her own drafts through that same filter before turning them in. She didn't get much more praise, but the redlines got shorter. Over time, she noticed her manager was trusting her with more client-facing tasks.

It wasn't a dramatic transformation, but Adrienne gradually learned how to hold her own in a high-pressure environment, and how to not take the feedback personally.

Time to Shine

Adrienne didn't become best friends with her manager. She still got nervous before big presentations and played catchup plenty of times. But down the road when she left that role, she knew how to work under pressure, think ahead, and deliver work that held up under scrutiny.

It wasn't a perfect experience, but it stretched her, and that stretch stuck in the most positive way.

Case Study 3: Two Days, One Delay, and an Unexpected Partnership

Stage Setting

Rory was an operations associate who managed supply logistics for a consumer goods company. She kept things running smoothly: on time, on budget, and with minimal drama. One of her vendor contacts was particularly reliable, and over time, their email exchanges developed a friendly, no-nonsense rhythm and easy rapport.

Spark Moment

A week before a major product launch, Rory noticed one of their regular shipments hadn't arrived. She double-checked the system, but there was no clear update, and emails to the vendor's shared inbox were going unanswered.

She briefly considered sending her manager panic signals. Instead, she reached out directly to the one contact she'd always had smooth interactions with. They'd only emailed about timelines and invoices before, but something told her to try.

Path to Thrive

Rory picked up the phone and called her contact. They'd never spoken outside of scheduled updates, but she had a hunch.

Sure enough, the contact had already flagged a possible mix-up at the warehouse. "We're seeing some scan issues on our end. I think this might be caught in a batch delay," he said. "Let me loop in someone on our side to dig in and keep you posted."

Time to Shine

The issue was ultimately resolved, the product launch did well, and things went back to normal. But Rory didn't see her job quite the same way. That one collaboration shifted her perspective: even quiet, behind-the-scenes relationships could have a real impact, sometimes right when it matters most.

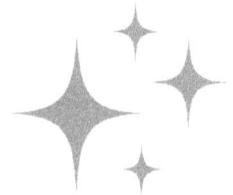

Here's how to tune into the lessons, connections, and unexpected value every relationship can bring.

1. True to You Check-In

How you navigate relationships often says more about you than the other person. When interactions feel tense or off, it's easy to fall into reaction mode. But taking a moment to reflect helps you respond with clarity—not emotion—and build a reputation rooted in professionalism, not tension.

Something to Try:

After a tricky or uncomfortable interaction, ask yourself:

- Was I trying to win the point—or understand the person?
- Did I assume the worst, or pause to consider their perspective?
- What's one small shift I can make next time to keep the connection intact, even if we disagree?

Moments of friction can be positive turning points.

2. Stay in Sync Tracker

Relationships don't keep themselves in shape; they need check-ins, attention, and care. By being intentional about who you're connecting with (and how), you create stronger foundations and avoid letting the important stuff fall through the cracks.

Something to Try:

Use your Work Journal to keep a running list of connections:

- Reliable Allies: People you trust who make space to stay connected, even casually.
- Challenging Dynamics: Track moments when you've tried to improve the tone or flow.
- Under-the-Radar Collaborators: People in your orbit that you haven't really engaged with yet.

Think of this as a playlist: curate it with purpose, keep it fresh, and don't let the best tracks get buried at the bottom.

3. Shine Prompt

Strong work relationships don't require grand gestures but steady signals that say: "I see you, and I value what you bring." Small actions, especially during challenging dynamics, can open doors that emails and meetings never will.

Something to Try:

Try one of these small but meaningful actions:

- Highlight someone's contribution, especially if they're not in the spotlight.
- Ask a thoughtful question that invites someone's insight or experience.
- If something feels off, tap a trusted colleague for perspective on how to reconnect.

The best connections are built in quiet moments, not big moves, and it's on you to make the first move.

Last Call Spark

Every connection shapes you—some in obvious ways, others in whispers and curveballs. Whether they lift you up or challenge your patience, people help refine your voice, sharpen your style, and show you who you are. That's growth you can't get alone and is well worthy of your investment.

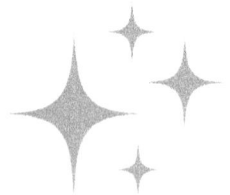

Chapter 12

Celebrate Wins, Learn from Losses: Both Successes and Setbacks Are Essential Parts of Your Growth

Landing a big win feels incredible, but how often do you take a pause to celebrate it? And when something doesn't go your way, do you move forward or let it weigh you down? True growth comes from embracing both highs and lows with equal intention.

Wins reinforce what's working, while setbacks provide lessons that make you better. The key is to process both productively. This chapter breaks down how to acknowledge your achievements without complacency and extract value from every challenge without getting stuck in the disappointment.

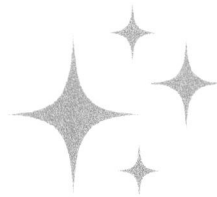

Confessions of a Recovering Perfectionist

For the longest time, I thought success was achieved by getting everything just right. A typo in an email? Mortifying. A fumbled answer in a meeting? Pure disgrace. I was convinced that if I dissected every misstep enough, I'd never make the same mistake twice.

The irony was that my obsession with avoiding mistakes sometimes held me back more than the mistakes themselves. I swung between extremes—first by improvising too much, then overcorrecting by over-preparing—all in an attempt to be, well, perfect. I finally realized that perfection couldn't possibly be achievable. Getting better, however, was. Now, I don't just focus on polishing every detail; I focus on making progress, learning as I go, and giving myself permission to be human.

Why High-Fives and Faceplants Both Matter

★ **Wins Reinforce Your Strengths**
Acknowledging your achievements helps you see what's working and build momentum. Don't just brush off success—own it.

- **Losses Provide the Blueprint for Your Next Move**

  Setbacks aren't failures; they're roadmaps. Each challenge reveals what needs fine-tuning, making you sharper for the next round.

- **Resilience is Built in the Balance**

  Success isn't about only winning—it's about learning how to navigate both triumphs and failures with grace and strategy.

- **Recognizing Progress Fuels Motivation**

  Celebrating even the small wins keeps you engaged and inspired to keep pushing forward.

- **Your Career is a Collection of Both Wins and Lessons**

  No one remembers just the highlight reel. The moments of struggle shape your journey just as much as the successes—embrace both.

My Own Lesson: A Hard-Won Victory with a Humbling Twist

As a contract manager, I handled high stakes deals, but one stands out as both a career high and a sharp lesson.

I was working on an eight-figure agreement with a notoriously difficult client, one that my much more senior predecessor hadn't been able to close. Every term, every condition was scrutinized, debated, renegotiated over months. When we finally reached the finish line, the client signed. The deal was done. I felt on top of the world. I had done it!

Then came the gut punch.

When I submitted the signed contract for processing, legal found an error: a small but critical term was missing. 100% my mistake. This meant we had to redo the "final" version and go back for re-signature.

It created unnecessary risk and complications, never mind my utter embarrassment when I had to report this to my management and get their help fixing it. I had no choice but to own it.

The Lesson Earned

That deal was a huge learning opportunity. Yes, wins deserve to be celebrated, but losses demand to be learned from.

I was so focused on getting the deal across the finish line with flourish that I skipped an important step. Wins and mistakes aren't opposites – they're two sides of the same coin.

A mistake doesn't erase a win, just like a win doesn't mean there's nothing to improve. The real success is learning how to do both.

Case Study 1: One Broken Link, One Big Wake-Up Call

Stage Setting
Erin, a marketing assistant, was leading her first solo email campaign for a product launch. She was solidly in her wheelhouse, having supported multiple campaigns like this before with other leads. She double-checked the design, crafted a catchy subject line, coordinated with every team, and hit send.

She was very proud of the work. Until the next morning.

Spark Moment
Her boss called her into a meeting. One of the main links in the email was broken. Instead of sending customers to the product page, it led to an error message. There was an instant flurry of emails wondering what was going on.

Erin's stomach dropped. The mistake was small, but the impact was big—and her boss didn't sugarcoat it.

Path to Thrive
Erin owned the error immediately. Then she took a

breath, regrouped, and suggested a fix: a follow-up email with the correct link and a small incentive for early buyers. With support from her team, she sent it out the same day.

Afterward, she created a pre-send checklist to avoid future errors—not just for herself, but to share with the broader team. The mistake stung, but it also sharpened her instincts.

Time to Shine
The campaign wasn't perfect. But Erin's response showed something even more valuable: she could take accountability, recover fast, and keep the project moving.

When she apologized to her manager again during their 1:1, the reply surprised (and reassured) her: "I'd rather work with someone who learns from mistakes than someone who pretends not to make any."

Case Study 2: When Confidence Outran Preparation

Stage Setting
Jasmine, a junior project coordinator, had always been told she was a great communicator. She felt comfortable in meetings, spoke clearly, and had a knack for connecting with people. When she was asked to lead a client check-in on an ongoing project, she didn't stress.

She blocked off time to prepare but figured it wouldn't be complicated: present a few slides and a quick status rundown. She knew she had it covered.

Spark Moment

The meeting didn't quite go as planned. As Jasmine was going through the project status, the client asked about one of the dependencies, and she stumbled. She hadn't reviewed the latest project timeline in detail and gave an answer that didn't line up with what the team had discussed the day before.

Her manager had to jump in to correct the confusion. The moment passed quickly, but Jasmine felt it. She hadn't bombed, but she hadn't delivered, either.

Path to Thrive

Afterward, her manager pulled her aside and said, "I know you have the skills, but for these kinds of calls, you have to be 100% ready."

Jasmine realized she'd underestimated how much time it actually took to be ready – not just to sound confident, but to be confident. Before the next meeting, she spent more time with the team, walked through the updated deck, and asked questions to make sure she understood the details behind the slides.

Time to Shine

At the next client call, Jasmine handled a smaller portion of the agenda. She still felt nervous, but when a question came up, she was able to respond clearly and keep things moving.

It wasn't flawless, but it was solid. Afterward, her manager gave her a "good job" nod that confirmed her prep had paid off.

Case Study 3: How Owning the Win Changed the Game

Stage Setting

Taylor, a communications analyst, had been on the job less than a year when her team was asked to prep the CEO keynote for a high-profile company event. When a senior team member got pulled away at the eleventh hour, Taylor stepped in, drafting talking points, managing edits with the executive team, and helping shape the final delivery.

The keynote went smoothly, and the CEO was very complimentary. The team breathed a sigh of relief with high-fives all around.

Spark Moment

At the next team meeting, the credit went mostly to the returning senior member, who had polished the final version but hadn't done the bulk of the work. Taylor smiled, nodded, and said nothing.

Inside, she felt deflated. She hadn't expected a standing ovation, but she hadn't expected to feel invisible either. Part of her wondered if it was just what happened when you were early in your career: you do the work; others get the credit.

Path to Thrive

Later that week, during her 1:1, Taylor brought it up: "I realized I haven't really talked about how much of that project I took on while things were shifting," she said. "I know I'm still new, but I'm proud of how I handled it."

Her manager nodded. "You're right. You stepped up, and I didn't call that out the way I should have. Thank you for saying something."

It wasn't a fix-all, but it made Taylor understand something: people aren't always tracking your accomplishments. Sometimes, you have to share the scorecard yourself.

Time to Shine

For the next big campaign, Taylor volunteered to send out weekly recap emails that highlighted progress, next steps, and contributions (including her own) to her manager and the full project team.

She didn't frame it as credit but clarity, and it helped others easily see her contributions. She started building her reputation as a solid performer on the team.

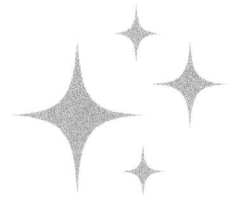

Let's make space to appreciate the highs, learn from the lows, and grow from both.

1. True to You Check-In

Everyone handles wins and losses differently: some people dwell, some brush them off, and some barely acknowledge them at all. But your reaction to success and setbacks can teach you a lot about yourself. Recognizing what energizes you and what deflates you helps you navigate your career with clarity and confidence.

Something to Try:

Think back to a recent win and a challenge (big or small). Instead of just labeling them "good" or "bad," go deeper:

- What felt energizing about my win? Was it the recognition, achievement, or problem-solving?
- What felt frustrating about the challenge? Was it a skills gap, a misstep, or a situation beyond my control?
- What does this tell me about what I value and where I thrive?

Wins and losses can serve as mirrors reflecting what drives and stretches you.

2. Stay in Sync Tracker

It's easy to focus on individual moments and forget the bigger picture. But real growth isn't about single events but patterns. Spotting recurring wins and challenges helps you understand what's working, what's evolving, and what needs attention.

Something to Try:

Draw out a simple Growth Grid in your Work Journal with three sections:

- Strengths in Motion: What keeps showing up as a win? What am I consistently good at?
- Works in Progress: What keeps challenging me? Where am I seeing slow but steady growth?
- Energy Drainers: What keeps frustrating me or feeling off? Is it something I can improve, shift, or let go of?

Over time, you'll start noticing patterns you can act on.

3. Shine Prompt

Wins and lessons don't always come in big, obvious packages. Sometimes, the biggest breakthroughs come from small, daily realizations, the ones you'd forget if you didn't capture them.

Something to Try:

Take one minute to capture two quick thoughts:

- One thing that worked today: a small win, progress, or good moment.
- One thing that taught me something: a challenge, mistake, or unexpected insight.

Drop them in your Work Journal, phone notes app, or scribble them on a sticky note. No deep dive needed—this is a quick snapshot to remind yourself that every day brings both progress and perspective.

Last Call Spark

Success isn't a straight line at all; it's a dance of momentum, reflection, and resilience. Wins fuel your momentum. Losses sharpen your edge. When you treat them both like teachers, you turn every experience into a notable milestone, and every step you take adds to the blueprint of your progress.

Thrive and SHINE

N

Navigate Change

One thing is guaranteed in your career: change will come for you, ready or not. Sometimes it's a thrilling new opportunity; other times it's a curveball that knocks the wind out of you. Either way, how you handle change will define your ability to thrive.

Here's the secret: The moments that feel the most uncertain are often the ones that shape you the most. Whether you're facing a career pivot, an unexpected setback, or a leap that scares the hell out of you, learning to embrace change with clarity, confidence, and resilience is what turns obstacles into building blocks.

In this section, we'll break down how to reframe setbacks into opportunities, take strategic pauses that prevent burnout, and use boundaries to stay grounded instead of overwhelmed. And because you're not here to just "go with the flow," we'll explore how to make change work for you, not against you.

I won't sugarcoat it: change can be messy. Believe me, I've been blindsided by it more times than I can count! But every time, I've come out the other side stronger, wiser, and a little bolder. And so will you.

Let's navigate change together. You can turn it into your greatest advantage.

Chapter 13

Every Detour Hides a Gem: Find Opportunities in Surprises and Setbacks

No one plans for a career curveball. A role shift, a layoff, a project failure—these moments can feel like roadblocks. But what if they were redirections? Some of the best career moves come from situations we never would have chosen, forcing us to step outside our comfort zone. This chapter is all about shifting your mindset to see setbacks as opportunities, adapting with confidence, and making the most of unexpected changes that might just lead you to something even better.

Confessions of a Backseat Driver to the Universe

I had my career planned down to the decimal. Every next step? Mapped out. Every milestone? Pre-programmed.

Controlling my day-to-day work with perfectionist tendencies wasn't enough; I was intent on designing my entire career path. I fought unexpected detours, resisted change, and tried to force my plan into reality. But life had other ideas. Eventually, I learned (not easily) that the best opportunities weren't the ones I meticulously planned for. They were the ones I never saw coming. Turns out, the universe might actually know what she's doing.

Why Life's Left Turns Lead You Right

★ **Detours Reveal Strengths You Didn't Know You Had**

Some of the best skills you develop come from navigating unexpected challenges. The roadblocks shape you as much as the victories.

★ **Change Forces Growth, Whether You're Ready or Not**

When things don't go as planned, you adapt, innovate, and get creative. Every unexpected turn teaches you something valuable.

- **What Feels Like a Setback Can Be a Setup**
  Sometimes, the opportunities you didn't get would have held you back from something better. Trust that reroutes often lead to better destinations.

- **Resisting Change Wastes Energy—Lean Into It Instead**

  Fighting what's already happening doesn't change it. Instead, shift your mindset and ask, "How can I make this work for me?"

- **A Straight Path is Forgettable—Twists Make it Worth Telling**

  The best career journeys are rarely linear. The surprises, pivots, and unexpected wins make your path uniquely yours.

My Own Lesson: From Crushing Blow to Career Glow

I thought I had it all figured out: after thriving in my role and stacking big wins, I was in the running for a high-exposure chief of staff position with the company president.

It was hush-hush, but everything was aligning. I was so locked in on this dream job that I glided through my current role, and things started slipping. This wasn't intentional, but I wasn't pouring the same energy into my work.

Then, the rug got pulled. A leadership shuffle meant the role vanished overnight. Worse? My "private" campaign turned out not to be so private. My entire leadership knew, including my boss. The worst? There was a RIF going on, and suddenly, I was on the layoff list with 30 days to find a new job—or be out.

Panic. Fear. Humiliation.

Then, almost by chance, I landed a different role—not glamorous, not high-profile, but solid. And guess what? That job opened the path to the next move, which was one of the most challenging, rewarding, and career-defining phases of my life.

The Lesson Earned

I thought if I wanted something badly enough, planned for it hard enough, and went all in, it would happen. Wrong.

I was so fixated on the next step that I lost sight of where I was standing, and that was a mistake that could have cost me big. Your best shot at any opportunity is always tied to how well you're showing up right now.

That detour didn't feel like a gift at the time, but it was. The plans we obsess over aren't always the ones that take us where we're truly meant to go.

Case Study 1: How the Wrong Job Opened the Right Door

Stage Setting

Anya, a junior software engineer, had been working on a high-profile app project, her chance to prove herself. She embraced the challenge, pushing herself to be the best on the team.

Spark Moment

Then, the project was suddenly canceled. Instead of moving to another innovative initiative, she was reassigned to an internal support team focused on maintenance and bug fixes. The work felt repetitive, and she struggled with the feeling that she had been sidelined.

For weeks, she did the minimum, quietly frustrated that her career had stalled before it had even started.

Path to Thrive

One day, she overheard two junior engineers struggling with an issue she had solved months ago. Without thinking, she stepped in to explain the fix in a way that made sense to them.

From then on, the questions kept coming. Anya found herself teaching, troubleshooting, and mentoring without realizing it. She had always thought of leadership as something that came later in a career, but she was already stepping into it.

Time to Shine

By the time performance reviews came around, management had noticed. Instead of moving her back to a coding-heavy role, they offered her a technical team lead position.

At first, she was surprised; wasn't she supposed to be proving herself as a developer? But the truth was, she had been proving something even bigger.

The experience taught her that not all career growth is linear. Sometimes, the path you didn't choose is the one that reveals your greatest strengths.

Case Study 2: The Fire Alarm that Set Off a Wake-Up Call

Stage Setting

Natalie was an event planner finally getting her big break: a large-scale corporate retreat for a Fortune 500 client. It was the kind of assignment that could put her on the map.

This was exactly the time of event she had been preparing for. She was confident that it would be a huge success, and she felt fully in control.

Spark Moment

At the event's opening reception, things started to slip. Fast.

A vendor shipment was missing, and no one had been assigned to track it—so there was no ETA. The caterer showed up with half the staff needed for passed hors d'oeuvres. The electrical setup wasn't configured for the DJ's system, and the tech crew was scrambling for backup cables.

When a decorative candle triggered the fire alarm mid-program, it wasn't just a surprise. It was the breaking point. Guests were confused, the team panicked, and Natalie realized: when prep isn't locked airtight, anything that can go wrong will.

Path to Thrive

There was no smoothing over what had happened. The client was disappointed, and there was a lot of apologizing to do. Natalie stepped aside to let her manager lead the rest of the event.

At first, she questioned whether she was even in the right field. She had always defined success as flawless execution, and this experience shook that.

But instead of walking away, she leaned in. She started rebuilding her planning systems and her mindset. She tightened risk management and rigorously stress-tested every event. More importantly, she stopped aiming for "perfect" and started preparing for real life.

Time to Shine

A few months later, Natalie was given another shot—another high-stakes client, another big event. It didn't go perfectly: a vendor mix-up threw the schedule off, and tensions ran high behind the scenes.

But this time, Natalie didn't freeze. She stayed calm, made quick calls, adjusted timelines, and kept the client informed and calm.

It wasn't the kind of success she would've aimed for before, but it was the kind that mattered. She realized she didn't need things to run perfectly to feel proud. She knew she could handle whatever came her way.

Case Study 3: How Moving Boxes Unpacked New Possibilities

Stage Setting

Kat, the office manager at a mid-sized law firm, thrived on structure. She ran a tight ship—inventory, facilities, scheduling—everything had a system. It wasn't glamorous work, but she took pride in how smoothly things ran.

So when the firm announced it was relocating to a new space across town, Kat was irritated. The layout was unfamiliar, the workflows would change, and the whole thing felt like a disruption she didn't ask for. And then came the kicker: she was asked to lead the move.

Spark Moment

At first, Kat treated it like a task list: file the permits, schedule the movers, check the boxes. But things got complicated fast: construction delays, last-minute furniture swaps, lease negotiations, IT rewiring.

That's when something clicked. Instead of reacting to problems, she started planning around them. She juggled timelines, managed vendors, coordinated departments, and somehow kept it all moving.

What she'd seen as a headache turned out to be something she was genuinely good at—not just organizing but orchestrating.

Path to Thrive

Once the move was complete, there was a positive shift for Kat. A few colleagues asked for her input on space planning and vendor contracts. Her manager looped her into a new facilities rollout to get her take.

The move had surfaced a different side of her capabilities, and it made her start thinking differently, too. She realized she liked solving messier problems, not just maintaining order. She started saying yes to small side projects she once would've avoided, curious to explore beyond her comfort zone.

Time to Shine

A few months later, when another department needed help coordinating a hybrid office setup, Kat offered to assist with the logistics. The work wasn't glamorous, but it still got noticed. In a team meeting, her manager called out her role and thanked her for stepping in.

That moment stuck with her. She was starting to see herself as someone who could go beyond just keeping things running and actually help shape how things worked in the first place.

Even if the route changes, there's still plenty to learn along the way. Let's reflect on what the detours are teaching you.

1. True to You Check-In

Change can feel disorienting, especially when you're early in your career and still learning how things work. Whether it's a canceled project, a shift in team priorities, or something bigger like a budget cut or company restructure, even small detours can shake your footing. But how you respond in those moments can reveal more about your values and instincts than any perfect plan. Reflecting on what happened helps you stay steady, no matter how things shift.

Something to Try:

Think back to a recent curveball, big or small. Ask yourself:

- How did I handle it in the moment?
- Did my reaction reflect the kind of professional I want to be?
- What did this show me about what matters most to me?

Even when plans change, you can still move forward with purpose—and you might be surprised by what that leads to.

2. Stay in Sync Tracker

It's easy to miss your own progress when change feels messy. But if you pause to reflect on how you've adapted—over time—you might see just how resourceful you've become. Tracking your reactions and takeaways helps you build a stronger sense of control in uncertain moments.

Something to Try:

Create a "Turns I Took" section in your Work Journal. Whenever something unexpected comes up, write:

- What changed?
- What did I do in response?
- What came out of it that I didn't expect?

This becomes a personal record of how you're growing through change—not in spite of it, but because of it.

3. Shine Prompt

You don't need to love change, but building a little flexibility into your day makes the big stuff easier to manage. When you practice shifting your mindset in small ways, you develop confidence that lasts—even when plans flip upside down.

Something to Try:

Next time something changes unexpectedly, try one of these tactics:

- Name it: Simply acknowledge, "Okay, this is different than I expected." That small pause helps you respond, not react.
- Look for one thing that's still working and lean into it.
- Ask yourself: *"Is there something I can learn or take from this that might help me later?"*

Change doesn't always feel good in the moment—but it often leaves you stronger, sharper, and more ready for what's next.

Give *Yourself a Minute*

You're allowed to feel it. Step away, cry in the car, scream in a pillow, whatever you need. Then breathe, reset, and rise.

Last Call Spark

Detours aren't distractions—they're where discovery lives. The setbacks, side paths, and surprises? They often reveal parts of yourself and your journey you never would've planned but now wouldn't trade. Sometimes the "wrong" turn leads you exactly where you're meant to go.

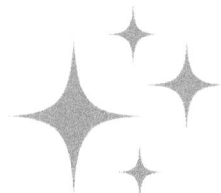

Chapter 14

Pause, Pivot, and Propel Forward: Regroup and Make Your Next Move Count

We often think success is about moving forward at all costs, but what if the best next step is actually pausing? In high-pressure moments, taking time to assess and recalibrate isn't a sign of indecision—it's a strategic move. Whether you're navigating a career shift, recovering from a setback, or rethinking your goals, knowing when to pause, pivot, and propel forward is essential. This chapter shows you how to reassess with clarity and move forward with intention so that your next step is the right one, not just the fastest one.

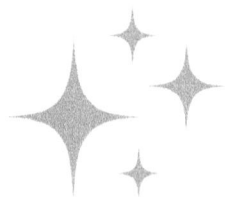

Confessions of a Procrastination Virtuoso

I like to think of myself as the rare breed who genuinely loves change—no moss growing on this stone. Maybe it's my short attention span, or my fly-by-the-seat-of-my-pants streak wrapped around a deep love of control and perfection. I dive into the new fast. And once I do? I've already lost interest in whatever I was doing before. That's when procrastination creeps in; my mind is already somewhere else. It feels efficient in the moment. Until it doesn't.

Why Smart Pauses Keep You Moving Forward

★ **A Pause Isn't a Full Stop—It's a Strategy Reset**

Pausing lets you zoom out and make intentional decisions instead of reacting impulsively. Smart professionals know when to step back before stepping up.

★ **Pivoting is About Adjusting, Not Starting Over**

If the current path isn't working, shift direction instead of abandoning the journey. Small adjustments can lead to big breakthroughs.

- **Momentum Comes from Thoughtful Action, Not Just Speed**

  Moving fast without a plan can lead to burnout. The most effective progress happens when you balance reflection with decisive steps forward.

- **Overanalyzing Leads to Inertia—Decide and Move**

  Strategic pauses are powerful, but overthinking keeps you stuck. At some point, action beats analysis.

- **You Don't Need the Whole Roadmap—Just the Next Step**

  You don't have to see the entire journey before you begin. Take one step forward, and the path will unfold.

My Own Lesson: Hitting Fast Forward and Running into Reverse

I was working under a manager who wanted his fingerprints on everything: every slide, every sentence, every decision. He was smart and experienced, but I felt boxed in. I was itching to move faster, think bigger, and take the reins.

When I found out I'd be transferring to a new team with a new manager, I quietly celebrated. It felt like a fresh start. Mentally, I packed my bags and left early.

In my head, I'd already moved on. I wasn't trying to drop the ball; I just figured I'd be out before due dates. And if I'm being honest, I tapped right into my procrastination habits. I convinced myself there was no harm in slowing down, when really, I was just avoiding the work I didn't want to do under a manager I was eager to leave.

But the transition dragged. And by the time I snapped back into gear, it was too late. My deliverables weren't up to standard, and my performance review reflected it. Worse? My new manager saw it, too.

What was supposed to be a fresh start now came with baggage—and a credibility gap I hadn't planned on.

The Lesson Earned

I thought I was moving forward, but I'd actually hit pause without meaning to.

Transitions don't erase what comes before. In this case, detaching too soon while pausing without intention ultimately created loose ends that followed me into what should've been a clean slate.

Now I know: a real pivot is done with intention, clarity and integrity. Even if you're itching for what's next, how you leave matters just as much as where you're going.

Case Study 1: How Holding Her Ground Nearly Held Her Back

Stage Setting

Paige, a junior communications assistant, had finally found her rhythm. After a year of refining her workflows, she had a clean system and clear ownership over her projects, and it felt like she was trusted to deliver.

Then a new hire joined the team—same level, similar role—and was paired with Paige on a new campaign. From day one, this teammate was energetic, outspoken, full of bold ideas, and eager to get involved in everything. Paige tried to play it cool, but inside, she felt thrown. Her once-clear lane now felt cluttered.

Spark Moment

At first, Paige pulled back. She stopped offering ideas during brainstorms and handled tasks on her own to avoid overlap. But it didn't help. In fact, she started missing small details, things she used to catch without thinking.

One afternoon, while reviewing feedback on a campaign brief she'd written, the new teammate caught an error that had almost slipped through. Paige sat there, annoyed...and then surprised. She wasn't just frustrated with the change. She was letting it get in her way.

Path to Thrive

Re-engaging wasn't easy. Paige still felt bruised—like the work she had quietly built up was suddenly being overshadowed.

But deep down, she knew this wasn't working. She didn't want to keep missing details or resenting someone who was, in reality, just doing their job.

She made a quiet choice to explore collaboration and real teamwork. She proactively invited her teammate to regularly scheduled check-ins and working sessions. It felt awkward at first, but over time, they found a better rhythm: checking in early, dividing tasks more clearly, and learning when to lean on each other's strengths.

Time to Shine

In the end, their campaign landed well, not because either of them had all the answers, but because they figured out how to meet in the middle.

The new teammate didn't derail Paige's work after all. But resisting the change? That almost did.

Case Study 2: Letting Go of Perfect, One Line at a Time

Stage Setting

Sienna, a junior architect, had just landed her first major assignment: designing a multi-use space for a new urban development. She poured herself into every detail, creating sleek renderings and an ambitious layout that showed off everything she'd learned so far.

It felt like her big moment.

Spark Moment

Then halfway through, the client slashed the budget.

Her carefully built vision unraveled. Materials, design features, layout details—gone. The lead architect announced they'd have to rethink everything. Sienna was crushed. She barely spoke in the next team meeting and avoided looking at her original plans. She felt like the project had been gutted, and with it, her momentum.

Path to Thrive

For a few days, she floated through the meetings, half-listening, half-resenting. But one evening, while staring at a blank sketchpad, she started playing around with an alternate layout—tighter footprint, more multipurpose design, scaled-back finishes.

It didn't feel exciting, but it felt possible.

She brought the draft in the next day. Her team didn't cheer, but they didn't dismiss it, either. They built on it. Slowly, Sienna got back in the flow—not with the plan she loved, but with one that worked.

Time to Shine

The project moved forward with her scaled-down design at its core. It didn't feel like a huge win, but it didn't feel like a loss anymore, either.

On the day the plans were finalized, Sienna found herself flipping back to her original renderings. What once felt like a career-defining vision now looked... overdesigned. Like it was trying too hard to impress.

The new version didn't have flash, but it had function. It worked. And that felt good.

Case Study 3: The Step Up that Shook Her Steady Ground

Stage Setting

Ava had been in her coordinator role at a media company for about a year when a job posting opened up in another department—one that looked more creative, more visible, and more aligned with what she really wanted to do.

She wasn't sure she was ready, but she applied anyway—and got it. Everyone congratulated her. She felt proud... and nervous. This was it, the exciting pivot she had been waiting for.

Spark Moment

Within a few weeks, the shine wore off. The new team moved fast, used unfamiliar systems, and had little time for onboarding. Ava struggled to keep up. She kept rereading emails, missing cues in meetings, and second-guessing everything.

She felt disoriented and ashamed. This was supposed to be a leap forward—but all she felt was stuck. Her confidence tanked, and for the first time in her short career, she wondered whether she'd made a mistake.

Path to Thrive

One morning, instead of trying to power through, she did something that felt counterintuitive: she paused. She started asking more questions. She requested a few one-on-ones just to learn how others handled things. She started keeping a notebook of what she didn't understand—then followed up after hours to fill in the gaps.

She wasn't thriving. But she was slowly starting to stabilize. She let go of the idea that she had to impress everyone immediately and focused instead on just *learning the job*.

Time to Shine

Ava's move didn't unlock some instant glow-up. In fact, the months that followed were slow and sometimes discouraging. But she stuck with it.

One day, after finishing a project that had totally stumped her a few months earlier, she looked back at her notes—pages of acronyms, half-formed questions, and follow-up reminders—and realized how far she'd come.

She wasn't ahead of the curve yet. But she wasn't lost anymore, either.

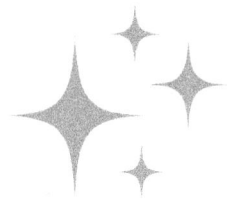

When things shift, take a beat. These reflection prompts will help you move forward with clarity—not just speed.

1. True to You Check-In

When things get hectic, you may not always get to hit pause, but you can take a beat to check in with yourself. Even a quick mental reset can help you shift from reacting on autopilot to responding in a way that feels clear and grounded.

Something to Try:

Next time things start to swirl, ask yourself:

- Am I moving just to keep moving—or is this the direction I want to go?
- What matters most right now: clarity, calm, or progress?
- If I can't slow the world down, how can I steady myself from within?

It's like tapping the brakes just enough to see the road ahead.

2. Stay in Sync Tracker

Transitions create motion—and mess. Loose ends can linger, and people may be unclear about what's finished and what still needs you. Tidying up even the small stuff helps clear space and gives you more control as you shift into what's next.

Something to Try:

Start a "Loose Ends & Launch Pads" list in your Work Journal:

- What can I finish, hand off, or close with a quick note or update?
- What needs a final touch so I can truly move on?
- What's still in limbo that's worth resolving—now or soon?

You don't need to tie it all up with a bow—a knot is sometimes enough.

3. Shine Prompt

Changes don't always come with a map, but every move you make can help you regain your footing. Small, clear steps build confidence, especially when the bigger picture is still forming.

Something to Try:

Choose one action that helps you reclaim some forward momentum:

- Ask one question that brings you more clarity
- Cross off one lingering task—even if it's small
- Jot down what's taking up mental space to make room for what's next

Every step you take is a reminder: you're still driving, even if the road has changed.

Stick This on Your Monitor

"I am allowed to take up space and still be learning." Write it. Repeat it. Let it anchor you when your doubt gets loud.

Last Call Spark

You don't need the perfect plan—you just need to stop, breathe, and shift with purpose. Every pause creates space for clarity. Every pivot is a chance to realign. And when you move with intention, even the messiest change becomes your launchpad.

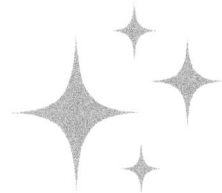

Chapter 15

Grounded and Growing: Leverage Boundaries to Anchor and Elevate

Boundaries aren't limitations; they're the foundation that lets you expand without losing yourself. And no, you don't need a senior title to start using them. Early in your career, it can feel like you're supposed to say yes to everything, be endlessly available, and push through no matter what. But without any guardrails, that pace becomes unsustainable fast.

Setting boundaries is about making intentional choices: how you manage your time, communicate your capacity, or protect space to actually think and do your best work. Even small shifts like blocking calendar time, asking for clarity before jumping in, or turning off notifications when you need focus can all make a big difference.

This chapter unpacks how boundaries, even quiet ones, help you stay grounded while growing into bigger challenges —and why learning to use them early on sets you up for long-term success.

Confessions of a Workaholic Without Borders

I used to think boundaries were for people who wanted to slow down. I didn't. I wanted to shine. That meant saying yes to everything, answering every late-night ping, and proving I could juggle it all without breaking a sweat. Work wasn't just something I did; it became how I measured my value. And the more I gave, the more essential I felt, until I couldn't tell where my job ended and I began.

Why Boundaries Build Bridges to Growth

★ **Boundaries Protect What Matters Most**
Saying no to distractions means saying yes to the work, relationships, and goals that align with your values.

★ **Limits Help You Play the Long Game**
Burning out today won't get you further tomorrow. Sustainable success comes from knowing when to push and when to pause.

★ **Saying No Makes Room for Bigger Yeses**
The more intentional you are with your time, the more opportunities you can seize that truly align with your goals.

- **Respected Boundaries Earn More Respect**
  People take cues from how you treat yourself. Holding firm on your limits shows that you value your contributions.

- **Structure Creates Freedom—And Peace of Mind**
  The right boundaries give you the space to take risks, explore new ideas, and grow without feeling stretched too thin.

My Own Lesson: All In and All Out of Balance

When my boss took a C-level job at a new company, I was the one person he brought with him. It felt like a crown jewel moment: bigger title, better pay, major visibility. I saw it as a once-in-a-career launch, and I wasn't about to mess it up.

Boy, did I go all in. I said yes to everything: 4:30 a.m. calls with Europe, late-night meetings with Asia. Cancelled plans, skipped meals, stopped working out. Work was the only thing I had room for.

While I was getting things done, I wasn't building anything for myself. I didn't deepen cross-functional relationships. I didn't make space to reflect or develop my own vision. I didn't set any boundaries because I thought boundaries were for people who weren't "all in."

Then one day, my boss was suddenly gone in a snap. I had a hard epiphany: I had built my entire identity inside someone else's orbit. I had visibility, but no foundation. I had a title, but no leverage.

After all that work, I had nothing I could really claim as mine.

The Lesson Earned

I used to think boundaries were limits. But what I didn't see is that the absence of boundaries isn't freedom. It's exposure.

If I'd carved out even a little space for reflection, for direction, for my relationships, I wouldn't have felt quite as lost when the structure around me shifted.

Boundaries wouldn't have slowed me down. They would've made me stronger. These days, I don't confuse being all in with giving it all away.

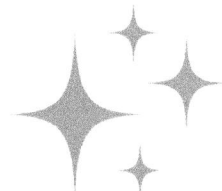

Case Study 1: How She Stepped Back to be Seen

Stage Setting

Lena, a customer success rep at a software company, was known for jumping in wherever needed. She answered every ping, took on every stray task, and made herself indispensable.

She prided herself on being helpful, and truthfully, she liked being liked. She feared that saying no or setting limits would make her seem uncooperative or replaceable, so she said yes. To everything.

Spark Moment

One week, her calendar was packed with back-to-back calls and urgent requests. She stayed late every night, convinced she was holding everything together.

Then a teammate she often helped asked if she'd review their workflow again "really quick." Lena said yes automatically—then realized afterward she'd missed her own project deadline.

The kicker? The teammate thanked her—and then sent the final version straight to their manager without mentioning Lena's help at all.

She wasn't mad. She was just... done. She realized she was burning herself out to please people by doing their work for them.

Path to Thrive

At first, Lena thought about pulling back completely, but that didn't feel right either. Instead, she started small. She blocked one hour a day for her own work. She paused before responding to every request.

And when she said no, she tried something new: she didn't overexplain. She simply said, "I'm at capacity right now. Let's figure out another plan."

It felt awkward at first. But the world didn't collapse. People adjusted. And surprisingly, there was no blowback.

Time to Shine

One afternoon, a teammate dropped her a message:

"Hey, I figured it out. Thought you'd be proud."

Lena was proud, not because she had fixed anything—but because she hadn't.

That small moment confirmed it: she didn't need to overextend to be appreciated. The more she trusted herself to set reasonable boundaries, the more others stepped up, and the more space she had to do the work that added to her growth.

Case Study 2: Inbox Full, Energy Empty

Stage Setting

Jade, a junior marketing associate, was known as someone who got things done. She handled slide decks, last-minute edits, and urgent asks without complaint. She was reliable—but also invisible.

When a big cross-functional campaign kicked off, she was pulled in to "support the team." The strategy lead asked her to take notes, coordinate meetings, and organize materials. Jade agreed—then quietly watched as others took the lead on creative direction, messaging, and high-impact decisions.

Spark Moment

After a few weeks of juggling low-level tasks, Jade noticed a familiar pattern. She was in every meeting, on every email thread, and constantly pulled into last-minute requests—everything from formatting decks to chasing down approvals.

Then one Friday afternoon, her manager forwarded a "quick request" from the strategy lead: could Jade pull together research slides by Monday?

Jade stared at the message. She could do it, yes, but she realized that, once again, she was being treated as the catch-all helper. Not a contributor with focus or potential.

She took a breath and replied: "I'd be happy to contribute early next week, but I'm at capacity this afternoon. Also, if you're open to it, I'd love to support the positioning work next. That's more where I'd like to grow."

Path to Thrive

She expected pushback or a plea. But instead, the lead replied: "Fair enough. Let's loop you in on the messaging next week."

It was a small shift, but it changed everything. Jade still did her share of coordination, but she was now included in creative discussions more often. She stopped auto-defaulting to "yes" and started asking where she could add the most value.

Time to Shine

By the end of the campaign, she had positively contributed to both copy and visuals for the launch assets, had learned a lot, and had improved in skills areas she wanted to strengthen.

She realized that boundaries didn't block opportunity. When used wisely, they made room for it.

Case Study 3: When a Rotation Recalibrated Everything

Stage Setting

Ivy, a financial analyst at a large healthcare company, had just wrapped a high-intensity stint on a revenue forecasting task force. The pressure had been nonstop, but she'd thrived on the pace and assumed she'd be fast-tracked to a strategy team next.

When she was assigned to a six-month rotation in internal reporting, managing stakeholder updates and routine dashboards, she was frustrated. No strategic modeling. No big decisions. Just spreadsheets and check-ins.

It felt like a detour. And not the good kind.

Spark Moment

A few weeks in, Ivy was still trying to overachieve—sending detailed analyses no one asked for, building dashboards with extra layers that slowed things down, and volunteering to "polish" reports that were already final.

One afternoon, she noticed something. A colleague submitted a bare-bones update, got a quick "thanks" from the director, and that was that.

Meanwhile, Ivy had just spent hours crafting a 10-tab workbook that barely got opened.

That's when it hit her: She wasn't adding value. She was just adding... more.

She realized her internal drive to prove herself was becoming a distraction for everyone around her, including herself.

Path to Thrive

Ivy started setting boundaries—not with her team, but with herself. She blocked time for focused work, stopped obsessively rebuilding reports, and declined "extra" work that wasn't part of the rotation's scope.

It wasn't easy to slow down. But she gradually realized she was doing her best work by working smarter, not harder. Her accuracy improved. Her updates became cleaner. And her confidence got steadier.

Time to Shine

By the end of the rotation, Ivy hadn't made a big splash. No standout wins, no calls from senior leaders.

Her final report was clean, her numbers were sharp, and a teammate casually asked, "Hey, can I use your format? It's a lot easier to follow."

It wasn't the kind of recognition she used to chase, but it meant something.

By setting small parameters for herself—less overdelivering, more clarity—she'd become more accurate, more efficient, and more trustworthy.

She wasn't blindly running on overdrive. Her feet were firmly planted, and she was still stretching onwards and upwards.

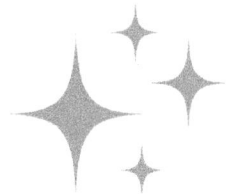

Here's how to create the structure you need to grow without feeling boxed in.

1. True to You Check-In

During transitions, everything can feel like it needs your full attention right now. And in early roles, you might not always have control over your workload or what's asked of you. But even then, you do have the ability to notice when something is pushing your limits. You can pause just long enough to decide how you want to show up.

Growth isn't just about simply taking on more. It's about learning what stretches you in the right ways, and what stretches you too thin.

Something to Try:

The next time a new ask or responsibility lands on your plate, take a quiet moment to check in:

- What's my gut telling me about this?
- Am I stretching in a healthy way, or starting to overextend?
- Is there a small adjustment I can make to manage this better, even if I can't change the ask?

Even if you can't control the situation, you can still stay connected to what matters most to you, and that clarity can keep you grounded through any shift.

2. Stay in Sync Tracker

You don't need full authority to set clear expectations. Keeping others informed about what you're focused on or what you need help with builds respect and helps prevent misunderstandings before they happen. Communicating your capacity isn't about saying no; it's about being thoughtful and proactive.

Something to Try:

When you're feeling overwhelmed, start a "Focus Signals" log in your Work Journal. Use it to reflect on moments where you communicated what you were working on or asked for clarification when things felt overloaded. Ask yourself:

- Did I clearly share what I was prioritizing or juggling?
- Did I give others a heads-up when something needed more time or support?

- Was there a way I could have spoken up with more confidence or clarity?

These signals don't need to be big; they just need to be steady. They'll go a long way in helping others work better with you.

3. Shine Prompt

You may not always get to choose your workload, but you can choose how you manage your energy. And sometimes, just one small act of focus or self-respect in a day can help you feel like you're still steering the wheel, even when the road gets bumpy.

And here's the real secret: when you protect your energy in smart ways, you're not just avoiding burnout: you're creating space for the kind of growth that actually moves you forward.

Something to Try:

Pick one way to protect your capacity today without needing to make a big announcement:

- Set a quiet boundary, like turning off notifications during deep work

- Decline a non-critical meeting invite with a quick, respectful note
- Use five minutes to regroup instead of powering through when you feel drained

These small choices build the muscle of self-trust, and that's what helps you grow in a way that's sustainable, strategic, and meaningful.

Last Call Spark

Smart boundaries don't box you in—they lift you up. When you create space for what truly matters, you're not limiting your growth, you're designing it. Clear limits = deeper focus, stronger impact, and more energy for the things that move you forward.

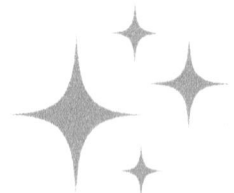

Chapter 16

Flex Your Wings and Flourish: Turn Uncertainty into Your Biggest Strength

Uncertainty isn't a weakness—it's an opportunity. Some of the most successful professionals aren't the ones who always know what's next but the ones who can adapt and thrive in evolving situations. Whether it's a role shift, an industry change, or an unexpected challenge, knowing how to embrace uncertainty allows you to grow in ways you never imagined. This chapter is about leaning into the unknown, staying flexible, and developing the mindset that turns uncertainty into your career advantage.

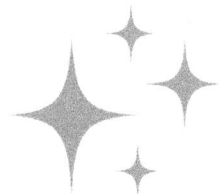

Confessions of an OCD Over-Planner

To compensate for my natural inclination to improv and procrastinate, I pushed myself in the complete opposite direction. I became a meticulous planner: color-coded calendars, backup plans for my backup plans, timelines with sub-timelines. I thought if I planned hard enough, I could outmaneuver uncertainty.

But life, however, does not care about my spreadsheets. The biggest, most game-changing moments in my career were not on my carefully crafted roadmaps. Through many repeated lessons, I've realized that planning is great, but gripping the plan too tightly is just fear in disguise. Now, I still love a good checklist, but I leave room for the unexpected. I've learned that's where the magic really happens.

Why Letting Go Leads to Lift-Off

- **Overthinking is the Enemy of Action**
  Success doesn't wait for the perfect moment; it rewards those who take the leap despite uncertainty.

- **Your Best Moves Come from Embracing the Unknown**
  Some of the biggest career wins happen when you step outside the script and take a risk.

★ **Uncertainty is a Creativity Playground**
When the path isn't clear, you're free to innovate. The best breakthroughs happen when you allow yourself to experiment.

★ **Small Steps Lead to Big Wins**
You don't need to have everything figured out. Just start moving, and more clarity will come with action.

★ **Trust that You're Stronger Than You Think**
Every time you face uncertainty, you build resilience. You've done hard things before, and you'll do them again.

My Own Lesson: Lauded, Lost, then Lifted

I was on fire in my job: winning company awards, leading major initiatives, making a name for myself. Every day was a new win, and I felt unstoppable.

And then, everything changed.

We had a new executive heading up our department. My biggest advocates were out. My role started shifting in ways I couldn't define. The career path I'd been carefully building was suddenly meaningless.

I felt stuck. Unmotivated. Borderline depressed.

Then, an old colleague reached out. He'd just stepped into a leadership role and needed help on a project. Since I had unexpected bandwidth, I jumped in.

That one project led to another, and soon, I was working for him in a challenging, creative, and growth-filled role. Later, when he moved into a C-level position at another company, I followed into an even bigger role myself.

The plan I had was long gone. But where I ended up was so much better.

The Lesson Earned

I thought if I planned everything just right, I could control how it all unfolded. But when my beautiful roadmap crumbled, so did my sense of direction.

What I didn't expect was that the best parts of my career—the biggest growth, the boldest moves—came not from controlling the path, but from trusting myself enough to follow where it led.

I stopped chasing the perfect plan and learned to follow the momentum. Sometimes the detour is the greater plan.

Case Study 1: How Stepping in Turned into a Step Up

Stage Setting

Harper was a program assistant at a regional education nonprofit, supporting a workforce training initiative. She was good at her job, which was largely administrative support with some communications and project management tasks. She liked knowing what was expected and being able to check things off her list.

Spark Moment

When the program's lead coordinator left unexpectedly, things got murky fast. Her manager reassured the team it was "a short-term gap," but in the meantime, questions kept landing in Harper's inbox.

Where were the updated handouts? Who was running next week's session? Was the new curriculum design still on track?

At first, Harper tried forwarding the emails or asking someone else. But answers were slow, and she could feel things falling through the cracks.

Path to Thrive

Harper had two choices: play it safe or step up. She didn't have clear direction, but she started doing what she could.

She pulled what she knew from past notes and followed up with facilitators. She blocked time to update outdated documents and checked in with instructors proactively. She wasn't sure she was "qualified," but she did have context, and that turned out to be more helpful than anything else.

The pace was rough. Some days she felt way over her head. But slowly, things stabilized.

Time to Shine
Things didn't exactly calm down right away, but Harper no longer felt like she was chasing every answer or waiting for someone else to take the lead.

She had found a rhythm: following up, stepping in, helping others feel steady even when she didn't always feel that way herself.

She wasn't just keeping the work moving. She was moving differently too. And that shift was the catalyst she needed to level up.

Case Study 2: Out of Sight, Off the Radar

Stage Setting
Gwen, a junior accountant at a regional firm, had been doing well. She'd built good relationships, knew her workflows inside out, and liked the steady pace of her role. She was on a great career track.

When her partner got a job in another city, Gwen asked to work remotely. Her manager approved it, and she settled into her new home with relief.

No more commuting. No more small talk. No one popping over her desk mid-task. She was excited about this comfortable arrangement.

Spark Moment

At first, Gwen thought things were going fine. She was meeting deadlines, getting her deliverables in, and no one was chasing her down.

Working remotely made her feel fully independent, like she had total control of her time. And without the rhythm of an office to ground her, she let that independence stretch too far.

She didn't always reply to Slack messages right away. Sometimes emails sat a little longer than they should have. She still cared about her performance, but she hadn't made the effort to structure her day or enforce discipline on herself.

She was missing the habit of showing up as part of the team.

Path to Thrive

Gwen didn't crash and burn, but she didn't adjust either. Rather than find a new rhythm and really own her remote status, she defaulted to what felt safe: finishing her tasks, keeping her own pace, and staying in her lane.

She told herself she was fine, that she was still being productive.

But the more she avoided the awkwardness of reengaging, the more out of step she became, and the less she was thriving.

Time to Shine

As the weeks and months passed, Gwen was still doing her job, but she had faded into the background more than ever before. Her name didn't come up in conversations the way it used to.

She hadn't leaned into the new, unfamiliar, and uncertain situation. A few small choices could have made a big difference and set her up for success, but she never made them.

Choosing comfort is fine, as long as it's intentional and done with full awareness of the cost.

In Gwen's case, her passivity came at the cost of growth.

Case Study 3: The Dense Fog that Brought New Insight

Stage Setting

Nancy, a management consultant at a global firm, was great with deliverables. Give her a scope, a timeline, a framework, and she was in her zone.

She'd been staffed on back-to-back internal transformation projects, where the pace was clean, and the clients were clear. She'd gotten into a rhythm and was starting to feel confident.

Then came her first account assignment: a global consumer brand going through a messy executive shakeup and unclear priorities.

Nothing was defined. Stakeholders contradicted each other. Timelines kept shifting.

Spark Moment

Nancy tried to power through the confusion, producing detailed trackers, slide decks and reworked timelines to reflect the client's changing requests. But nothing seemed to land.

The leadership team kept asking vague questions she didn't know how to answer, and the senior manager on her team started quietly taking over the meetings.

Nancy could feel herself slipping into the background but had no idea how to regain her footing. She wasn't doing anything "wrong," but somehow, she still wasn't delivering what the situation called for.

Path to Thrive

The ambiguity stressed her out, and she worried she was damaging the account relationship. Nancy considered asking to be reassigned, but she knew that wouldn't reflect well on her.

Instead, she adjusted her approach. She stopped trying to solve everything mid-meeting and focused on clarity. She started doing better prep before meetings and solid follow-ups with crisp recaps afterwards. As her output improved in quality, her confidence grew, and she started to see that others were increasingly relying on her.

Time to Shine

There was no dramatic, defining moment, no huge breakthrough or big win.

But over time, Nancy started to feel more sure-footed. She worked smarter, spoke with more intention, and caught signals she used to miss.

The fog hadn't lifted completely, but she wasn't frozen in it anymore. She was learning how to move through the unknown, not by pushing harder but by flexing differently.

This account didn't get easier, but she definitely got better at navigating it.

Growth doesn't always feel graceful. Let's reflect on how to stretch without snapping.

1. True to You Check-In

When change happens, it's tempting to shrink back or just do what's expected. But those are also the moments when you have the chance to flex your wings, to test your strengths in new ways, even if you're not sure you're ready. Growth isn't about being fearless; it's about being honest with yourself and stepping forward anyway.

Something to Try:

Think back to a recent change, big or small. Ask yourself:

- What strengths helped me through it?
- Did I try something I hadn't done before, even if it felt uncomfortable?
- How did that stretch help me grow or show me what I'm capable of?

Note your reflections in your Work Journal to remind yourself that your wings get stronger every time you use them.

2. Stay in Sync Tracker

When you're in a stretch season, it's hard to tell the difference between growth and burnout. Sometimes it feels like you're flying, and sometimes you're flapping like mad and getting nowhere. That's why checking in with your direction matters so you know if you're actually building lift or just losing steam.

Something to Try:

Use a simple "Stretch vs. Soar" check-in to reflect:

- Stretching: Am I being pulled in too many directions? Am I running on fumes?
- Soaring: Am I leaning into opportunities that challenge me and feel meaningful? Do I feel energized—even if it's hard?

You won't always be soaring, but knowing the difference helps you recalibrate and stay on a growth path that works for you.

3. Shine Prompt

You don't build flight muscles by standing still. Even in early roles where you can't control the big picture, you can still find small, creative ways to grow, right where you are. These quiet moments of courage may not be flashy, but they're where confidence starts to take root.

Something to Try:

Look for an opportunity to stretch yourself, even in subtle ways:

- Offer a new idea in a group setting
- Volunteer for something just outside your comfort zone
- Take the lead on a small task you'd usually wait on

You don't need a big title to take up space. The more you stretch in meaningful ways, the more you'll trust your ability to rise.

Uncertainty *Is the Assignment*

Like it or not, change isn't a plot twist. It's the whole story. The trick is learning to move with it—curious, steady, wide open. Don't be afraid of it. You got this.

Last Call Spark

Change will test you, but it will also teach you. When you loosen your grip on certainty and meet the unknown with curiosity, you stop just surviving and start soaring. Flexibility isn't just how you adapt—it's how you rise.

Thrive and SHINE

E

Engage Meaningfully

There is one concrete truth in business (and in life): No one succeeds alone. The relationships you build, whether with colleagues, mentors, or unexpected allies, are the rocket fuel that will propel your career forward. But meaningful engagement isn't about collecting contacts or saying "yes" to everything. It's about showing up with intention, building trust, and knowing when to invest your energy—and when to protect it.

In this final section, we'll dive into what it means to truly engage: how to balance empathy with self-preservation, how to navigate feedback like a pro, and how to build relationships that uplift and empower you (without draining you).

The strongest careers aren't built in isolation. They're built through the connections that challenge you, champion you, and remind you of what you're capable of.

You've laid the foundation. Now, let's build something even greater. Together.

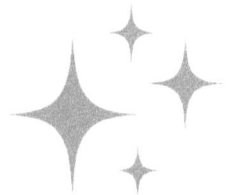

Chapter 17

Open Door, Not Open Floor: Be Available Without Losing Yourself

Being approachable and collaborative is valuable, but being constantly available? That's a fast track to exhaustion. If you feel stretched thin by endless requests, meetings, and interruptions, it's time to set some parameters that protect your focus without shutting people out. This chapter looks at how to create an "open door" approach that allows for meaningful engagement without sacrificing your time, energy, or priorities.

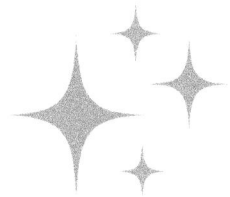

Confessions of a Reformed Go-To Girl

For years, I was the human equivalent of an emergency hotline: always on, always ready, always saying yes. And I loved it. It made me feel indispensable.

I was proud to be the one fixing everything at work: tasks, crises, last-minute asks. I thought being the person who handled it all made me valuable, but in reality, it made me overextended and overwhelmed. The hardest lesson I ever learned? Real impact doesn't come from saying yes to everything; it comes from knowing when to say no.

Why Smart Accessibility Wins Over Constant Accessibility

- **Being Selectively Available Protects Your Best Work**

  You don't have to answer every request immediately. Setting limits ensures you have the time and energy for high-impact tasks.

- **Flexibility Builds Trust, Burnout Breaks Trust**

  Being adaptable makes you valuable, but overextending yourself drains energy. Smart professionals know when to be accessible and when to focus.

★ **Boundaries Help You Deliver at Your Highest Level**

Constant interruptions reduce the quality of your work. Protecting your time allows you to show up fully for what matters most.

★ **Being Present is More Important Than Being Available**

You don't have to be online 24/7 to be reliable. When you set clear expectations, it helps people respect you and your time.

★ **Your Energy is a Resource, So Spend It Wisely**

If you say yes to everything, you'll have nothing left for the work and people that matter most. Guard your energy like it's your most valuable asset,because it is.

My Own Lesson: Second Banana to Solo Flight

Back when I was an executive assistant, I lived by one rule: always be available. I handled everything: calendar chaos, last-minute travel, surprise coffee cravings. If my boss or my team needed something, I was already halfway done.

I thrived on being the go-to. I ran on responsiveness and lived for the quick save. It boosted my self confidence (ok, my ego too) to no end.

But somewhere along the way, I blurred the line between being helpful and being consumed. My time wasn't mine. My wins weren't mine. I'd become so tied to someone else's success that I stopped investing in my own.

Then came a promotion opportunity. I wanted it, but I honestly panicked. I was stepping away from everything I'd used thus far to define my success.

My turning point? Realizing that my impact didn't have to come from being everyone's answer at all hours. It could come from choosing where and how I showed up.

I took the leap, and to my surprise, got the promotion. It wasn't seamless, but it was freeing. I started engaging with more purpose and less pressure. And I discovered I had a voice, not just a role.

The Lesson Earned

For a long time, I thought being indispensable was the goal. The more people counted on me, the more valuable I felt. But the harder I worked to be everything to everyone, the less I showed up for myself.

Turns out, real impact isn't about saying yes to every request. It's about knowing how to show up when it counts, even if you can't always control when or how.

Sure, there are still days I have to be "on" more than I'd like. But now, I focus on being present, prepared, and strategic with my yeses.

You can't be a lighthouse if your bulb's always burning out.

Case Study 1: Green Light Thinking, Red Light Moment

Stage Setting

Sabrina, a junior editorial assistant at a publishing house, was eager to move beyond logistics and be seen as a creative thinker.

She prided herself on showing up in meetings: offering ideas, volunteering to help, and raising her hand when things stalled. She thought she was being helpful and proactive. But others sometimes saw her as too quick to jump the gun.

Spark Moment

During a team review, a peer presented a campaign draft she'd been working on for weeks. Before the discussion even opened up, Sabrina launched into feedback: alternate headlines, layout suggestions, taglines. She was so excited that she didn't notice the room had fallen quiet.

Later that day, Sabrina's manager asked for an unscheduled 1:1. He shared: "I got a note that your feedback in the meeting was a little over the top," he said. "It came off like you were trying to take over, not collaborate."

Sabrina was stunned. She thought she was showing initiative, but now it seemed like she'd stepped on other people's toes. She was confused and embarrassed.

Path to Thrive

Her manager guided Sabrina to start paying closer attention to how she showed up in meetings, what she said, when and why she said it.

One tactic he suggested was taking more notes during meetings, which would naturally give others more time to speak while allowing her room to digest the information before diving in with ideas. This took practice, but it started working. She was developing better listening skills instead of anticipating when she could say her piece.

Time to Shine

A few weeks later, while reviewing a team draft, Sabrina spotted something unexpected: an edit that closely mirrored an idea she'd shared quietly in a previous meeting.

No shoutout, no spotlight, but the idea had stuck.

It was a real-time reminder that it wasn't important to be the loudest. It was about being heard clearly at the appropriate time.

She was learning what open doors were really for: knowing which ones matter and walking through them with intention.

Case Study 2: How Playing It Safe Became Sitting It Out

Stage Setting

Didi was a business development rep at a fast-growing SaaS startup. She hit her daily counts, met deadlines, stayed on task, and never stirred the pot. Her inbox was clean, calendar full, and numbers solid. She figured not being called out meant she wasn't causing problems. That had to be a good thing.

She wasn't trying to be distant. She just preferred to keep things simple: head down, job done, repeat.

Spark Moment

Over coffee one day, a former mentor asked how things were going. Didi mentioned a teammate who'd just been tapped to help lead a new client initiative—someone who had joined after her. "She's just...everywhere," Didi said. "Not sure how she gets pulled into all this stuff."

The mentor raised an eyebrow. "What do you want to be pulled into? What's next on the horizon for you?"

Didi froze for a second. She hadn't given that a thought—and hadn't put anything in motion to pursue the next thing.

Path to Thrive

After that conversation, Didi started to think about her own presence and participation a little differently.

When people asked for input in meetings, she stopped saying, "I'm good with whatever." When someone shared an update in Slack, she responded with a real comment. When a client meeting landed on her calendar, she prepped questions in advance instead of just note-taking in the background.

Nothing flashy—just more visible.

Time to Shine

A few weeks later, a senior rep on the team asked Didi to help prep content for a big pitch to a new prospect. Because she had started showing up and engaging, it was natural for her to be included in more activities that could open up new opportunities.

Didi hadn't reinvented herself. She had just opened the door—and let herself be seen.

Case Study 3: When Being Everywhere Led Nowhere

Stage Setting

Jaime, an HR coordinator at a mid-sized recruiting firm, prided herself on having a pulse on anything and everything. She was on every Slack channel, took notes in meetings she wasn't required to attend, offered help across departments, and made a point to stay looped in on every team initiative.

This approach felt like a strength. She was helpful, visible, and in the mix. She assumed the more she showed up, the more valuable she seemed.

Spark Moment

During an internal systems rollout, Jaime unexpectedly hit a wall. She had inadvertently joined three different working groups tied to the rollout, none of which were actually part of her role. Meanwhile, a time-sensitive benefits communication project—one she was responsible for—was still sitting in draft form.

During their check-in, her manager reviewed the status of her workload and said, "You're always jumping in, which I appreciate. But you need to prioritize what we really need from you right now and deliver strong."

Jaime felt her face getting hot. She thought being visible was the win, but it was starting to look more like a distraction.

Path to Thrive

Jaime took a hard look at her calendar. She'd filled it with meetings and messages that made her feel busy, but not necessarily effective.

She quietly stepped back from a few working groups, turned off unnecessary notifications, and started blocking time to focus on her core responsibilities. It felt strange not being everywhere but also freeing. It dawned on her how much bandwidth was really needed to finish the work that truly mattered.

Time to Shine

Her benefits rollout landed cleanly, on time, and easy to understand. Her manager gave her a simple but meaningful note: "This is great work. Nice job."

Jaime realized that being accessible didn't mean showing up everywhere. The real impact came from choosing where to focus and knowing when to step back so her best work could shine through.

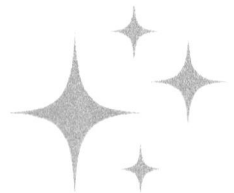

Availability is a skill. These checkpoints will help you stay accessible without being overwhelmed.

1. True to You Check-In

Engagement isn't about being the office help desk or a mysterious figure who only surfaces for mandatory meetings. It's about finding the right rhythm between being accessible and being focused.

If your work life feels like a revolving door, constantly spinning with interruptions, you might be too available. If people barely know what you're working on because you keep your head down, you might be too closed off.

The sweet spot? Open door, not open floor.

Something to Try:

Think back to your recent interactions and ask yourself:

- Did I show up in ways that added value, or was I just reacting to everything?
- Was there a moment where I could have contributed more but stayed quiet?
- Did I set a small but healthy limit that allowed me to focus?

If you're always on-call, tighten the door just a bit. If you're too under the radar, crack it open and let people see your work.

2. Stay in Sync Tracker

Being available is great. Being strategically available is even better. If you're always responding instantly, jumping into every conversation, or getting pulled into office debates that don't involve you, you're not actually engaging. You're just running on a treadmill.

On the flip side, if people hesitate to ask for your input because they're not sure if you're approachable, you might be missing chances to connect and contribute.

Something to Try:

Start a "Where I Showed Up" tracker in your Work Journal:

- What conversations did I engage in today?
- Did I speak up in the right moments or stay too much in the background?
- Was there a time I got pulled into something unnecessary and could have gracefully bowed out?

If you're feeling stretched too thin, find one area to dial back. If you're feeling invisible, find one way to step forward.

The goal? People should know they can count on you—but not expect you to be on-call 24/7.

3. Shine Prompt

Having an open door doesn't mean you're the office human suggestion box; it means people trust you to be present and engaged when it matters. If you've been overdoing it, *pull back just a little*. If you've been checked out, *step in a little more*. Small shifts can change the way you show up without burning you out.

Something to Try:

Choose one small way to engage meaningfully today:

- If you've been too reserved, speak up in a discussion or share an idea.
- If you've been too available, pause before jumping in—let others take the lead first.

- If you're always being asked for input, redirect a request to the right person instead of handling it all yourself.

Engagement isn't about being everywhere—it's about being in the right places, in the right ways.

Last Call Spark

Being helpful shouldn't mean being hollowed out. When you set thoughtful limits and show up with intention, you're not only protecting your energy, you're making space for deeper impact. Boundaries don't shut people out; they help you show up fully when it counts.

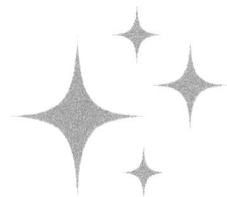

Chapter 18

Feedback Is Gold, Not Glitter: Use It to Shine Brighter

Feedback can feel like a confidence boost or a gut punch, depending on how it's delivered and received. The key is learning to filter the useful insights from the noise. Not all feedback is created equal, but when you know how to receive, apply, and even seek out constructive feedback, it becomes one of your most powerful professional tools. This chapter explores how to take feedback, both positive and critical, and use it to grow while maintaining your confidence and self-trust.

Confessions of a Feedback Flincher

I used to brace for feedback like it was an incoming missile. Even the kindest critique sometimes felt like a personal attack. On the flip side? I had zero hesitation dishing it out. I took pride in being direct and "helpful" (read: blunt).

It took me many cycles to understand that feedback isn't about proving a point. It's about growth, on both sides. Learning how to give and receive feedback with the right mindset changed everything for me. Now, I see feedback for what it really is: a gift, even when it stings to receive it, and a privilege to give it for someone else.

Why Feedback is Your Secret Weapon for Growth

- **Feedback is the Fast-Track to Excellence**

  You don't have to learn everything the hard way. Listening to feedback accelerates your learning curve and helps you refine your skills faster.

- **It's Not Criticism, It's a Competitive Advantage**

  The best professionals separate feedback from identity. Instead of taking it personally, they use it as fuel for improvement.

★ **Messy Delivery Doesn't Mean the Message Isn't Useful**

Not all feedback is perfectly framed, but there's often a nugget of wisdom in every critique. Train yourself to extract the useful parts and leave the rest.

★ **Giving Great Feedback Makes You a More Influential Leader**

Thoughtful feedback helps others grow while also sharpening your ability to communicate, mentor, and inspire.

★ **Your Willingness to Improve Defines Your Reputation**

Those who welcome feedback with curiosity instead of defensiveness are seen as adaptable, coachable, and ready for bigger opportunities.

My Own Lesson: When 360 Feedback Came Full Circle

I used to think I was great at giving feedback—honest, constructive, helpful. No fluff, no drama. When our team did 360 reviews for the first time, I took it seriously. I gave thoughtful comments and even included a note about one colleague who I felt was “a little too emotional at times.” I figured she’d appreciate the candor.

When I got my own results, they were mostly positive: some good input, a few areas to grow, nothing too surprising. But something was off for that colleague, the one I’d called emotional. She was clearly not okay.

I saw the shift in her. She withdrew a little, held back in meetings. Her spark was dimmed, and I knew I had played a part in that.

I hadn’t meant to shut her down. But the truth is, I’d taken something she brought to the team—her passion, her openness—and turned it into a flaw. I thought I was being direct, but I was actually being dismissive.

That experience changed the way I think about feedback. It’s not just about being honest; it’s about being responsible for the impact of what you say.

The Lesson Earned

I used to think the goal of feedback was to be helpful and honest. But looking back, I wasn’t just trying to help—I was trying to teach. And whether I meant to or not, that made me sound superior, not supportive.

At the same time, I wasn't always open on the receiving end either. I took in the comments, nodded along, but I wasn't fully listening; I was already drafting my defenses.

Many rounds of feedback sessions have taught me that feedback only works when both sides are open. Real feedback isn't just what you give or get – it's what you carry forward.

These days, I don't treat feedback like a lesson. I treat it like a bridge.

Feedback isn't your spotlight, and no one grows from being side-eyed and schooled.

Case Study 1: When Drowning in Drafts Sparked a Reset

Stage Setting

Penelope, an executive communications assistant at a consumer goods packaging company, had mostly handled internal newsletters and team memos. When she got tapped to help the company's SVP of Sales for a company-wide Town Hall deck, it felt like a huge opportunity.

She was excited and nervous. This wasn't just about graphics, grammar, or formatting. It was about tone, vision, and message. She wanted to get it right.

Spark Moment

Their first working session went off the rails fast. The SVP bounced between metaphors (The space mission! The Godfather! Battle at Normandie!), quoted competitors, dropped market stats, and launched into a stream of bold messaging ideas.

Penelope took notes furiously, trying to capture every idea, then spent hours trying to build a slide narrative that matched his energy. But every time she sent a draft, he'd come back with more. New angles. More ideas. No clear direction.

She realized she wasn't getting closer to what he wanted; she was just drowning in disjointed content.

Path to Thrive

After one particularly frustrating round of feedback, Penelope felt defeated. She sat staring at her laptop, unsure what version number she was even on anymore. The slides were a mess, and she was on the verge of tears.

She finally went to her manager and admitted she didn't know how to make sense of everything. Her manager then helped Penelope reframe the challenge: "You're not there to recreate all his ideas on paper. You're helping shape the message too. Speak up, drive the process, and help refine this so it's cohesive."

Together, they talked through how to structure the

next working session: start with specific questions and to-do items, clarify goals, and get reactions instead of open-ended ideas. Most importantly, Penelope practiced how to gently push back and ask for clarity.

Time to Shine

The next session wasn't perfectly smooth, but it was better. She led with the pre-designed structure, confirmed takeaways, and asked questions when things got murky.

In the end, the slides weren't flashy, but they landed well at the Town Hall. The SVP seemed genuinely pleased with the outcome.

Penelope didn't walk away feeling like a slide deck genius, but she had weathered the storm. She'd learned that feedback isn't something to passively accept or blindly follow—it's something to actively manage.

Case Study 2: The High Road Not Taken

Stage Setting

Autumn, a new legal assistant at a corporate law firm, joined with confidence. She was sharp, thorough, and used to fast-paced, high-standard environments. But from day one, things felt off.

She was paired with a longtime assistant, unofficially expected to "learn the ropes." But the division of work was murky, and the firm had no formal onboarding. Tasks overlapped. Expectations clashed. And no one clarified what success looked like in this setup.

Spark Moment

The tension was subtle—until it wasn't.

One afternoon, Autumn shared a revised intake process she'd cleaned up to make things more efficient. Her peer responded with: "Oh, I guess we're skipping approvals now?"

Autumn bristled. "Well, I figured someone needed to fix the lag."

From there, the exchanges escalated daily. Every suggestion became a veiled critique. Every edit felt like a correction. When they gave each other "feedback," it was couched in pleasantries but laced with bite.

"Just wanted to flag a few formatting inconsistencies again."

"Appreciate the help, though I had to redo most of it for clarity."

They weren't collaborating at all; they were sparring through email and redlines.

Path to Thrive

There was no confrontation, no formal blow-up. Just

a never-ending tennis match of passive aggressive exchanges.

And beneath it all, these two people were stuck in the same trap: trying to prove themselves, trying not to look weak, trying to be "right."

Neither trusted the other enough to have a genuine conversation. Neither of them stepped back to realize just how fast unclear, performative feedback can destroy even basic professional respect.

Time to Shine

Eventually, a resolution came. Alina's peer left the firm for another role. The parting was polite and professional, but that was a long-burnt bridge never to be repaired.

Alina stayed, and the tension lifted immediately. She could finally breathe. But there wasn't any satisfaction.

Looking back, she realized how much energy she'd wasted in a situation that had held her back. What she received as well as dished out wasn't feedback at all—it was one-upmanship.

She learned that real feedback, the kind that actually builds something, requires clarity, trust, and enough humility to own your part in the mess, even when the other person never does.

Case Study 3: When Soft Support Didn't Cut It

Stage Setting

Emily, a partner program manager at a global tech company, was juggling logistics for a massive hybrid summit: VIP speakers, high-stakes meetings, and multiple time zones. Her teammate was leading the internal content and session planning. It was a huge lift on both sides, and the pressure was mounting.

Emily could tell her teammate was starting to spiral, but neither of them had time to pause.

Spark Moment

A key internal stakeholder missed a critical deadline. Again. When Emily's teammate got the update, she snapped. She halfway yelled into the phone then slammed it down. Emily rushed over to her desk, and that triggered a loud, teary rant in the middle of their open office.

Emily tried to calm her down with quiet reassurances: "Totally fair... this is a lot... you've been holding so much." Her teammate finally took a breath, nodded and carried on, but the awkwardness in the room lingered.

Later, their manager pulled Emily aside. "I heard things got intense earlier. Can you talk with her about how things are going? I think she might hear it better from you rather than me jumping in."

Path to Thrive

Emily did not want to do any such thing. She wasn't comfortable with this situation, and she didn't want to make things worse. But she also knew her teammate's outbursts were starting to affect the team and the event.

The next day, she found a quiet moment and said, "I know how much you have on your plate and how frustrated you are, which is totally fair. But here we are. I don't want episodes like yesterday to take away from everything you are doing. Maybe sharing the workload sooner could help before it gets to that point."

It wasn't a perfect delivery. Her voice shook. But the message landed.

Time to Shine

The rest of the project wasn't magically smooth—there were still bumps and frustrations. But her teammate started looping others in earlier and asking for help as things came up. There were no more outbursts.

Emily realized feedback doesn't have to be flawless or forceful. Sometimes, the words that matter most are the ones you're scared to say but brave enough to speak.

Feedback can fuel your growth—if you know how to process and use it. Let's make that easier.

1. True to You Check-In

Feedback can feel like a spotlight—sometimes flattering, sometimes blinding. Whether it's praise that makes you squirm or critique that stings, your emotional response is your signal. Tuning into those reactions helps you shift from *"Am I failing?"* to *"What can I learn?"*

Something to Try:

Think of a recent moment when someone gave you feedback, formal or casual. Ask yourself:

- How did I feel in that moment? Defensive? Proud? Embarrassed?
- What part of it triggered that response? The words? The tone? The timing?
- Did I use the feedback or just survive it?

Jot down your thoughts in your Work Journal, not to overanalyze, but to start recognizing how you respond and why it matters. The better you understand your own patterns, the more power you have to use feedback as fuel, not friction.

2. Stay in Sync Tracker

Feedback isn't a one-and-done thing. It works best when it's part of a two-way conversation, through which input flows both ways and builds trust over time. The way you give and receive feedback can shape how people collaborate with you and how projects evolve.

Something to Try:

Start a "Feedback Flow" log in your Work Journal to reflect on recent interactions:

- Did I ask for feedback about something I genuinely wanted to improve?
- When I gave feedback, was it helpful and specific—or just an opinion?
- Did the exchange strengthen the working relationship—or make things feel awkward?

If feedback still feels intimidating, start small. Even saying, *"I'd love your take on this,"* creates an opening and shows you're growing into someone who seeks input, not just receives it.

3. Shine Prompt

Mastering feedback doesn't mean you have to deliver TED Talk–level insights or receive every critique with zen-like calm. It just means building your comfort with small moments of honesty, curiosity, and connection—one interaction at a time.

Something to Try:

Choose one micro-action to help you flex your feedback muscle:

- Ask for a gut-check. Try: *"Does this approach make sense to you?"*
- Clarify unclear input. Ask: *"Could you give me an example of what you mean?"*
- Offer something useful. Share: *"What you said in that meeting was super clear. I liked how you framed it."*

These moves build confidence, deepen trust, and turn feedback into forward motion.

Last Call Spark

Feedback isn't just about polishing. It's about progress. Whether it feels good or stings a little, it's a gift when you use it to grow, not shrink. The key is to stay open, stay grounded, and remember: the goal isn't perfection; it's evolution.

Chapter 19

Carry Kindness, Not Chaos: Empathy Without the Emotional Baggage

Kindness and empathy are powerful skills, but only when they're used wisely. It's easy to take on everyone else's stress, problems, and emotional weight without realizing it's draining you. So how do you balance being supportive without carrying burdens that aren't yours? This chapter helps you navigate the fine line between compassion and emotional overload, ensuring that kindness remains a strength instead of a source of burnout.

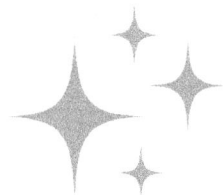

Confessions of a Fixer with the Feels

I used to think empathy meant going all in: feeling what others felt, fighting their battles, carrying their stress like a backpack full of bricks. Especially in my early days, I thought the best way to prove I cared was to absorb it all.

I didn't just root for people. I over-rooted. I became emotionally invested in their outcomes, even when the situation wasn't in my hands. I blurred the line between being supportive and being responsible. And the weight of that? Way too heavy to hold for long.

I've learned that feeling for someone isn't the same as fixing things for them. These days, I still show up with heart, but I keep both feet on the ground. Being kind with clarity is what keeps order, not chaos.

Why Kindness Is Your Superpower When You Keep Your Center

★ **Empathy Isn't a Full-Contact Sport**
You don't have to absorb people's emotions to support them. The most powerful empathy comes from being steady, not swept away.

- **Caring Doesn't Mean Carrying**
  You can care deeply without turning yourself into an emotional backpack. Holding space is generous but taking it all on is unsustainable.

- **Your Presence Is More Powerful Than a Fix**
  People don't always need answers, they need to feel seen. Staying grounded lets you offer support *without losing yourself in their storm*.

- **Protecting Your Emotional Energy Is an Act of Leadership**
  Emotional exhaustion doesn't serve anyone. Protecting your center helps you show up consistently, calmly, and compassionately.

- **Clear Is Kinder Than Overextending**
  You don't have to say yes to every request or soften every truth. Sometimes the kindest thing you can do is be honest, even when it's hard.

My Own Lesson: Misplaced Heartstrings that Led Me Astray

Early in my career, I worked as a placement agent at a staffing firm that focused on entry-level corporate roles: admin assistants, receptionists, clerks. I was still learning how to screen candidates and match them to open positions, and I loved having a job that helped people.

One day, I met a candidate who was kind, respectful, and eager to work: a single father trying to create a better future for his daughter. His resume was thin, and his office skills were limited, but I desperately wanted to help him succeed.

I prepped him for interviews, practiced his talking points, and sent him out for roles that, deep down, I knew were a stretch. But I couldn't help myself. I was all in on this guy. Every time he got rejected, I felt personally responsible. I kept pushing.

After a string of rejections, my boss pulled me aside. "You've sent him to multiple roles with no traction," he said. "We can't afford to send mismatched candidates. Our clients expect the right fit, every time."

My stomach dropped. Of course, my boss was right. In trying to help this candidate, I was risking my own credibility and the credibility of the firm. I had let my emotions take over my judgment.

I had to accept that empathy without alignment doesn't serve anyone. I had a final conversation with him, explaining that we didn't have roles that matched his current experience. He was disappointed, and I was genuinely sorry. But it was the right thing to do for everyone involved.

The Lesson Earned

Caring deeply doesn't mean carrying the full load. I thought support meant doing everything I could, even when it wasn't working. But support without clarity isn't helpful—it's enabling.

I learned that empathy needs reality checks. You can root for someone and still be honest about what's possible.

Kindness is most powerful when it's paired with perspective. You can only help when what you give actually meets what's needed.

Case Study 1: How a Safety Net Became a Snag

Stage Setting

Frankie, a marketing coordinator, had always been the helpful one, the person who took new hires under their wing and made sure everyone felt supported. So when a new intern started asking her for guidance, Frankie was happy to help.

At first, it was simple things: explaining a process, offering quick tips. But soon, the intern was leaning on Frankie for everything: feedback, proofreads, office politics, even help managing her confidence. Frankie found herself stepping in before she had a chance to figure things out for herself.

Spark Moment

One afternoon, the intern arrived at Frankie's desk, frustrated and near tears. Her manager had given her critical feedback, and she expected Frankie to step in to smooth it over, explain to their boss, and reassure Olivia that she was doing fine.

That's when Frankie realized that somewhere along the way, she had stopped being a mentor and started being an emotional crutch and unintentionally blocking growth.

Path to Thrive

Frankie knew she had to shift gears. Instead of immediately offering comfort or solutions, she started responding with questions:

"That's tough feedback. How do you think you should handle it?"

"What's your plan for addressing it?"

The change was subtle, but at first, the intern struggled. She hesitated. She wanted Frankie to keep fixing things for her. Frankie kept on this path.

Time to Shine

Frankie saw that the intern slowly started taking more ownership of her challenges. She still sought Frankie's advice, but she no longer expected her to carry the emotional weight of every setback.

Frankie still had moments where she almost stepped back into the fixer role. But she was learning that real mentorship wasn't about making things easier; it was about helping others build the muscles to do hard things themselves.

Case Study 2: When Being Nice Did No Favors

Stage Setting

Marina, a newly promoted account manager at a B2B software company, was known for being easy to work with. She was thoughtful in her emails, quick to thank people for their help, and always the first to offer support when her teammates were swamped.

She saw her role as the "glue" who made cross-functional collaboration smoother. But when it came to setting expectations or asking for something twice, she hesitated. She didn't want to come across as aggressive or rub anyone the wrong way.

Spark Moment

A few weeks before a key client renewal, things got bumpy. The client was asking for detailed ROI analysis on their current product portfolio. Marina had flagged it to the internal team, but her request had been vague: "If anyone has capacity, it would be amazing to get some insights pulled."

No one jumped in—who ever has capacity? And when the client followed up, Marina scrambled. She pushed answers from others a little too late and eventually patched together a good enough response with last-minute help from her manager.

Path to Thrive

With her manager's help, Marina started refining her asks. They even role-played follow-ups to help her practice being warm and direct. Instead of sending vague team pings, Marina shifted her language. She'd write:

"Can you send me the updated numbers by Thursday at 4PM?" or

"The client needs this to finalize their budget—can you confirm if you're the right contact?"

She wasn't trying to be tough. Just clear. And that made all the difference.

Time to Shine

The next client cycle wasn't flawless. There were still moments of tension, and Marina still caught herself over-apologizing.

But her clarity improved. The team responded more quickly. And the client did renew.

She didn't need to be the most experienced person in the room. Her job was to be the one who kept things on track. The more proactive she was, the more aligned the team was. Things were moving with less friction.

Case Study 3: Main Character Energy in Someone Else's Drama

Stage Setting

Ellie worked in a high-pressure, high-polish, high-competition corporate office—the kind of place where no hair was out of place and no sentence was unedited.

The managing director's assistant role was cursed. No one lasted. Then came the newest hire—bold, outspoken, and refreshingly unfiltered. She was brilliant, but loud about it. And in a world of quiet power plays, she didn't exactly blend in.

Ellie liked her. But the rest of the office? Not so much.

Because she had onboarded her and sat right next to her, Ellie became her unofficial therapist. Some of the complaints were legit. But Ellie started carrying the drama like it was her own.

Spark Moment

One day, Ellie vented to a VP she trusted—way too worked up over the whole situation. He listened, then said, "Why are you so upset? This isn't your problem. It's hers."

Oof. Instant, snap-out-of-it perspective shift.

Ellie realized she had let empathy turn into over-identification. She wasn't helping anyone—and she was draining herself. She needed to be kind without carrying the weight.

Path to Thrive

Ellie didn't stop caring, but she did start rebalancing.

She was more intentional about how much time she spent listening and soothing, knowing she couldn't keep absorbing someone else's stress. She stopped offering constant reassurance and started responding with neutral support:

"That sounds tough. What do you think you'll do next?"

She still listened, but no longer tried to fix.

When things escalated, she stayed kind, but didn't jump in.

Time to Shine

By making a conscious choice to stay grounded in her own role, Ellie learned to balance empathy with respectful boundaries.

What she had thought of as emotional support had led to her feeling ownership over something that wasn't hers.

That's not empathy. That's emotional entanglement.

You can listen, care, and advocate, but you don't have to bleed for every battle that isn't yours.

Here's how to show up with empathy without losing yourself in the process.

1. True to You Check-In

Kindness is powerful, but without limits, it can turn you into the office emotional sponge. Some people rush in to fix everything like they're auditioning for workplace superhero of the year. Others keep everything at arm's length to stay "professional," but end up missing real connection.

Neither extreme works. The key is to stay empathetic without hijacking your own peace of mind.

Something to Try:

Think back to a recent moment when someone at work vented, opened up, or got a little vulnerable. Ask yourself:

- Did I swoop in to fix it? Or absorb their stress like it was mine?
- Did I back away because it felt uncomfortable or "not my job"?
- If I had a do-over, what would I shift—engage more, or carry less?

You don't have to be a therapist. It's enough to be a human who listens, supports, and knows their limits.

2. Stay in Sync Tracker

Being a good colleague doesn't mean becoming a constant shoulder to cry on or a vault of emotional secrets. Emotional generosity is amazing, but it works best when paired with clarity about what's yours to hold and what's not.

Something to Try:

Use a quick "Kindness Filter" in your Work Journal after key interactions:

- Did I support without absorbing?
- Was I being kind—or defaulting to guilt?
- Am I starting to feel drained by conversations I don't need to own?

If you're always the one people go to, that says a lot about your empathy, but it also means it's time to check your emotional bandwidth. Being generous with your energy doesn't mean giving it all away.

3. Shine Prompt

Caring is a strength, not a job title. And trust me: the best kind of kindness is the kind that leaves both people feeling better, not just one.

Something to Try:

Try one small act that balances kindness with clarity:

- If you're the go-to helper: Instead of fixing, say: *"Want to talk through it together?"* You're offering presence, not pressure.
- If you tend to emotionally disengage: Reach out to someone who seems stressed with a simple *"Rough day?"* that can go a long way.
- If guilt is your autopilot: Tell yourself: "I'm being kind. I don't have to carry it all to care."

You don't have to drown in someone else's storm to be a good teammate. Sometimes, all it takes is throwing them a well-timed umbrella.

Frenemy Radar Is On

Not all smiles are safe. Trust your gut. Be kind, be cool, but don't give away your energy. You don't owe free access to everyone.

Last Call Spark

Empathy doesn't require absorbing everyone's emotions. You can lead with heart while protecting your peace. You can be kind and clear, warm and grounded. Putting yourself first makes your kindness sustainable.

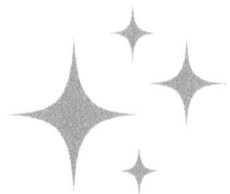

Chapter 20

Pack Your People Power: Build a Crew That's Got Your Back

If there's one truth about caree success, it's this: you can't do it alone. The people around you—mentors, colleagues, allies—can make all the difference in your growth and opportunities. But real networking is more than collecting contacts; it's about cultivating relationships that are meaningful, reciprocal, and lasting. This chapter shares ideas on how to build a strong professional community, nurture connections over time, and make sure you have the right people in your corner for every stage of your career.

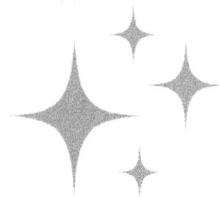

Confessions of a Vibe Reader

For a long time, I thought I was supernatural at relationship-building—because honestly, I was. Especially with people I clicked with easily. I leaned in, showed up, followed through, built camaraderie, earned trust.

If someone felt harder to connect with? I'd back off. Maybe not consciously, but I'd steer things toward surface-level. Shrug it off, chalk it up to different styles, and move on.

But here's the truth: the most powerful relationships aren't always effortless. Sometimes, the ones that challenge you are the ones you need to get right. And if you don't invest early, you might not get the chance to repair it later.

Connection doesn't have to be instant to be meaningful. Sometimes, the strongest bonds are unexpected.

Why the Right People Matter More Than the Most People

★ **Your Network is Your Springboard**
No matter where you are, strong relationships provide support, guidance, and game-changing opportunities.

- **Surround Yourself with People Who Challenge and Champion You**

  The company you keep shapes your ambition and success. Seek out those who push you forward, not just cheer you on.

- **A Powerful Crew Includes All Positions**

  You need a mix: mentors for wisdom, peers for shared growth, and rising stars for fresh energy and ideas.

- **Give More Than You Take and It Comes Back Around**

  The best professional relationships aren't transactional. Be generous with support, and you'll build long-term trust and loyalty.

- **Your Network Thrives on Genuine Connections, Not Just Contacts**

  The best relationships aren't about collecting names. They're built on trust, consistency, and mutual investment.

My Own Lesson: Lost My Badge, Found My Path

When I started at a new company as a marketing manager, I reported directly to the COO. The first stretch went smoothly enough: he seemed smart and structured, and I was eager to learn.

But soon, I could tell something was off. Our working styles didn't click. He started giving me unusually high-stakes assignments that went well beyond the ramp-up phase of a new hire. I worked hard, but it felt like I was always missing the mark. I wasn't succeeding at establishing a trust-based relationship with him.

On the other hand, I'd quickly built great rapport with the newly hired head of sales. We collaborated well, had mutual respect, and shared ideas easily. Apparently, that didn't sit well with my direct boss. Politics were brewing, though I didn't fully understand it at the time.

Eventually, things escalated. I was put on a performance plan, then let go. It felt abrupt and, frankly, baffling. I left that job stunned and confused.

Thankfully, that wasn't the end of the story.

A year later, that same head of sales reached out. He recommended me strongly for a role at his new company, and I ended up getting the job, which turned out to be one of the best roles of my career.

Years later, when he launched his own consulting firm, he invited me to work with him again.

He and I were different in many ways, but we shared respect and trust. What started as an unfamiliar working relationship turned into a long-term partnership that's lasted through multiple companies and chapters of my career.

The Lesson Earned

Office politics are real, but so is reputation, which is built on what you bring to the table and how you show up. I didn't win the short game, but I hit it out of the park with the long game.

People remember you—what you did, how you were—not just in the good moments, but in the tough ones too. While one door closed painfully, another opened down the line because someone saw my value and didn't forget it.

You can't always control your situation, but you can control how you approach relationships. The best opportunities come when you're acting with integrity and positivity.

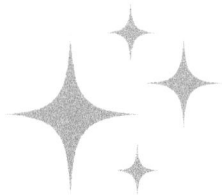

Case Study 1: It Takes a Village, Not a VIP

Stage Setting

Olivia thought she had a golden ticket: she'd built a friendly relationship with a well-connected executive at her company. She always made time to help, jumped in on stretch projects, and stayed visible and available. She figured her helpfulness would pay off down the line.

Spark Moment

When a coveted role was posted, Olivia was sure she was in the running. She'd worked hard and made herself indispensable to that one exec, who was one of the decision makers. But the promotion went to someone else. The real gut punch? The executive she'd supported didn't even speak up on her behalf.

She had poured her energy into one relationship but had neglected to grow a broader base of support or demonstrated her impact across the org. She was seen as helpful but not influential.

Path to Thrive

Olivia realized she had mistaken proximity for probability. Being in the room wasn't enough if no one saw her as an asset. She'd played the loyal supporter, not the strategic player.

She started diversifying her relationships, asking for feedback and input across departments, and contributing in ways that made her strengths visible beyond her closest allies. She understood it was important to be known for something meaningful.

Time to Shine

Olivia didn't get that promotion or a do-over, but got a great lesson learned. Having a reliable crew was about more than investing in connections; it was about creating a reputation that carried across teams, leaders, and situations.

Now, instead of waiting for someone to champion her, she was establishing her own credibility and making sure her career was powered by more than just potential favors.

Case Study 2: When Quiet Connection Turned Up the Volume

Stage Setting:

Dara was part of a high-speed team launching a bold new product line—something the company had never done before. The pace was intense, the stakes were high, and the team chemistry was solid. Everyone was stretched, but they were in it together.

Then came a shift: a new VP joined to lead a neighboring team with overlapping goals. She was well-regarded externally but brand new internally—no connections, no context. Her arrival created buzz and quiet tension. Would priorities change? Would roles shift?

Spark Moment:
While others kept their distance, Dara followed her instincts. She introduced herself, offered insights where it made sense, and engaged with curiosity and an open mind.

They didn't become instant allies, but over time, something steady formed. When the VP needed background, Dara shared it. When issues emerged, she flagged it early. Their relationship wasn't flashy, but it was solid.

Path to Thrive:
Months later, Dara's boss left unexpectedly, and the teams were merged. In the shuffle, she was moved under the new VP's leadership.

What could have been a scramble to start fresh turned out to be seamless. Dara didn't need to prove herself or earn trust from scratch; she already had a working relationship built on openness and consistency.

Time to Shine:
That early connection, formed without any master plan, became one of the most valuable of Dara's career. The VP grew into a trusted mentor and advocate who helped shape her journey in lasting ways.

Dara hadn't networked her way into that relationship. She'd simply shown up as her generous, grounded self and made space for collaboration.

And that people first, no agenda mindset turned out to be her real power move.

Case Study 3: Finding Her Fit without Losing Her Place

Stage Setting:
Caroline was hired as a sales assistant supporting one of the company's top-performing teams that was fast-moving, high-achieving, and proud of it. Their culture was intense but electric: aggressive targets, quick wins, big personalities, and a shared pride in being the best.

She liked a lot about her job: the momentum, the visibility, the fact that she was part of a team that got things done. She made herself indispensable, always on top of details, staying a step ahead, responding fast. The team liked her, and she liked being liked.

Over time, she started to feel a gap. The pace left little room for creativity. Independence was prized, but collaboration was minimal. She was developing her skills, but somehow, she was feeling less than fulfilled.

Spark Moment:
There wasn't a single turning point for Caroline—just a slow awareness.

The interactions she valued most weren't happening in team huddles or happy hours. They were in quieter moments, like with the analyst who took time to explain the numbers, the partner who invited her thoughts before sharing their own, the cross-functional contact who looped her in early instead of at the end.

They weren't high-profile, but they offered something different: space to learn, room to think, and a willingness to build together.

Path to Thrive:
Caroline began to shift, not away from the sales team but around it. She stayed engaged, kept doing her job well, and continued learning from the team's sharp instincts and fast moves. At the same time, she also started forming connections that brought out different strengths.

Those relationships didn't replace her existing ones; they expanded her world, and in doing so, helped her find a version of success that felt more like her.

Time to Shine:
Over time, those connections created new opportunities: a cross-functional initiative, a mentor who helped her map her next move, a deeper confidence in what she was capable of.

She still admired the energy of the sales team, and she knew she'd gained a lot by being part of it. But she no longer felt the need to mold herself to it completely.

People power, she realized, isn't about choosing one circle. It's about building the right mix that fuels you, stretches you, and makes space for your strengths to show.

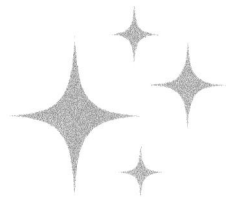

Your career is shaped by the people around you. Let's reflect on how to nurture those connections with care and intention.

1. True to You Check-In

Don't worry, not every work relationship needs to be deep. The strongest networks have a mix of people you trust, people who push you to grow, and people who may surprise you down the line. Staying mindful of where your energy goes helps you invest in the connections that matter most—without spreading yourself too thin.

Something to Try:

Sketch out three simple rings (bullseye-style):

- Inner Circle: People you trust, turn to, and grow with
- Middle Circle: Teammates, mentors, or peers who help you learn and stretch
- Outer Circle: Acquaintances you've crossed paths with, or people you'd like to know better

Ask yourself:

- Am I showing up for my Inner Circle, or taking them for granted?
- Is my Middle Circle still pushing me forward, or getting stale?
- Is there someone in my Outer Circle I want to reconnect with or reach out to?

The goal isn't to micromanage your network. It's setting a self-reminder to be intentional with your time and trust.

2. Stay in Sync Tracker

Relationships fade when you go radio silent until you need something. A simple check-in with no agenda can go a long way in keeping the connection real.

Something to Try:

Once in a while, scroll through your recent messages or contacts. Who haven't you talked to in a while? Choose one person from each of your rings and reach out casually.

No pressure. No pitch. Just something genuine like:

- "Hey, I was thinking about our last conversation. How's everything going?"
- "Saw your update—hope things are going well!"
- "Realized it's been a while. Want to catch up sometime?"

Let it be simple. Let it be human. That's how you keep relationships warm instead of letting them go cold.

3. Shine Prompt

Why it Matters:

The most meaningful networks aren't built with big gestures. They grow through thoughtful, everyday actions, especially when they're focused on giving, not just getting.

Your Practice:

Pick one small way to strengthen a connection or show support:

- Introduce two people who could benefit from knowing each other
- Share a resource or article someone might find useful
- Send a quick note to recognize someone's great work

These moves don't take long, but they leave a lasting impression and help you build a career filled with connection, not just contact lists.

Last Call Spark

You don't need a huge network; you need the one that's right for you. The people who challenge you, champion you, and walk beside you when things get tough? That's your crew. And when you show up for others the way you want to be supported, everyone rises—you most of all.

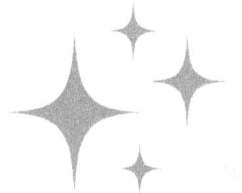

ACKNOWLEDGEMENTS

I didn't write this book because I had all the answers. I wrote it because I remembered the questions:

Who am I supposed to be? Am I doing enough? Am I even on the right path?

Over time, through more twists and turns than I ever could have predicted, I've learned that the best careers aren't built by following someone else's map. They're shaped by choices—sometimes bold, sometimes uncertain—that reflect who you are and who you're growing into.

The universe guided me—sometimes gently, sometimes with a push or a pull—toward a new chapter I never saw coming. I was that committed corporate girl who thought she had her path all mapped out. I never imagined I'd leave that world, let alone step into consulting, coaching, and now... writing a book.

This has been a long and winding road, and I didn't walk it alone.

To Gary—you are the love of my life and my grounding force. Your steadiness, your love, and your unwavering belief in me have carried me through so much. I am eternally grateful for you.

To Lola and Eden—you are bright, beautiful, wildly spirited souls. Being in your lives is one of my greatest joys. It's an honor to witness you becoming who you are.

To Maureen—your generosity empowered me to get this book across the starting line. I'm deeply thankful for your support.

To Heather—my kindred spirit and true ride-or-die. You've been with me through every step of this crazy adventure called life, and our friendship is a magical gift that keeps on giving.

To Manali—thank you for walking with me through the hard questions, the spiritual unraveling, and the clarity that followed. Your coaching helped me find my way back to myself.

To my mom—your strength, resilience, and perseverance have shaped everything I do. Thank you for leading by example and always being in my corner.

To the incredible team at Lucky Book Publishing—thank you for bringing this book to life with care, passion, and professionalism. I thank my lucky stars to have collaborated with you throughout this process.

To all the colleagues, mentors, clients, and team members I've crossed paths with—thank you for the lessons, the trust, the inspiration, and the growth. Whether we worked side by side or you let me walk alongside you on your own journey, I've learned something from each and every one of you.

And finally, to you, the reader: thank you for making space in your life for these pages. If something in here helped you feel seen, encouraged, or just a little more confident in your own shine, then that's everything I hoped for.

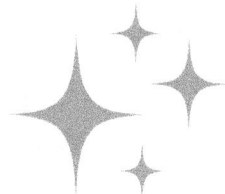

With heart,

Julee

ABOUT THE AUTHOR

Julee Sung is a career and life coach, speaker, and executive with over 25 years of experience across global enterprises, academia, and the nonprofit world. She's spent her career helping teams excel, ideas land, and people shine, even in the toughest environments.

Through her coaching practice, Julee empowers early-career professionals from all walks of life, including those rebuilding after personal or systemic challenges, to navigate the workforce with confidence and grace.

She lives in Los Angeles, California, where she finds joy in travel, beach walks with her rescue pup, breakthrough moments with clients, and showing up fully for the people she loves.

Instagram & TikTok: @julees94
Facebook: @juleesung94
LinkedIn: https://www.linkedin.com/in/juleesung/
Website: www.juleesung.com
email: julee@juleesung.com

thank you

Thank you for reading my book!

Dear Reader,

You've made it to the final page, but this isn't the end. Not even close. It all starts here.

By picking up this book, you did something very important: you chose to invest in yourself. You paused, reflected, and gave your growth the attention it deserves. Whether you're just starting out or charting a new course, I hope these pages reminded you that thriving isn't about being flawless—it's about being real, staying open-minded, and trusting that you've got what it takes, even when the path is unknown.

Thank you for spending your time and energy with me here. It means more than you know, and I am so grateful for you!

And hey—if this book made you think, laugh, nod along, or feel a little more seen, I'd love it if you left a quick review on Amazon or Goodreads. Your words could be the nudge someone else needs to take their own first step—and it truly helps others find Thrive and SHINE.

Keep showing up. Keep growing.
Shine on.

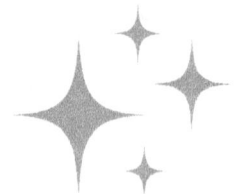

Warmly,
Julee

My Gratitude Gift to You

I'm beyond thrilled that you're here!

As my gratitude gift to you,
get FREE Access to the Audiobook of Thrive and SHINE by scanning the QR Code below or by visiting https://www.juleesung.com

www.ingramcontent.com/pod-product-compliance
Lightning Source LLC
Chambersburg PA
CBHW071544210326
41597CB00019B/3117
9781998287758